D1045613

25 BICYCLE TOURS
in the Twin Cities and
Southeastern Minnesota

250
BICYCLE TOURS
in the Twin Cities and Southeastern Minnesota

Erling Jorstad

Backcountry Publications
Woodstock · Vermont

Northfield Public Library
210 Washington Street
Northfield, MN 55057

94.99

An invitation to the reader

Although it is unlikely that the roads you cycle on these tours will change much with time, some road signs, landmarks, and other features may. If you find that such changes have occurred on these routes, please let the author and publisher know, so we may correct them in future editions. The author and publisher also welcome other comments and suggestions. Address all correspondence to:

Editor, Bicycle Tours
Backcountry Publications
P.O. Box 748
Woodstock, Vermont 05091-0748

Copyright ©1998 by Erling Jorstad

First Edition

All rights reserved. No part of this book may be reproduced in any form or by any electronic or mechanical means, including information storage and retrieval systems, without permission in writing from the publisher, except by a reviewer, who may quote brief passages.

Library of Congress Cataloging-in-Publication Data

Jorstad, Erling, 1930

   25 bicycle tours in the Twin Cities and southeastern Minnesota / Erling Jorstad

        p.   cm.

   ISBN 0-88150-408-4 (alk. paper)

   1. Bicycle touring—Minnesota—Minneapolis Metropolitan Area—Guidebooks. 2. Bicycle touring—Minnesota—Saint Paul Metropolitan Area—Guidebooks. 3. Bicycle touring—Minnesota—Guidebooks. 4. Minneapolis Metropolitan Area (Minn.)—Guidebooks. 5. Saint Paul Metropolitan Area (Minn.)—Guidebooks. 6. Minnesota—Guidebooks. I. Title

Published by Backcountry Publications
A division of The Countryman Press
P.O. Box 748, Woodstock, VT 05091-0748

Distributed by W. W. Norton & Co., Inc.
500 Fifth Avenue, New York, NY 10110

Cover photograph by Bob Firth/Firth Photobank
Cover design by Sue Wheeler and Hugh Coyle
Text design by Sally Sherman
Maps by Norman Sibley, © 1998 The Countryman Press

Printed in the United States of America
10 9 8 7 6 5 4 3 2 1

Acknowledgments

Thanks for great help in preparing this book to: Gary Wickes, John Marshall, Don Tarr, Bryn Geffert, Steve and Shelly Birkeland, and Ruth.

Also, thanks to the two fellow riders to whom this book is dedicated, J.D. Hanson of Shorewood, Minnesota, and Scottsdale, Arizona; and H.S. Hendrickson, formerly of Northfield, Minnesota, and now of Seattle, Washington—fellow riders, friends, critics. Both know why this book is dedicated to them.

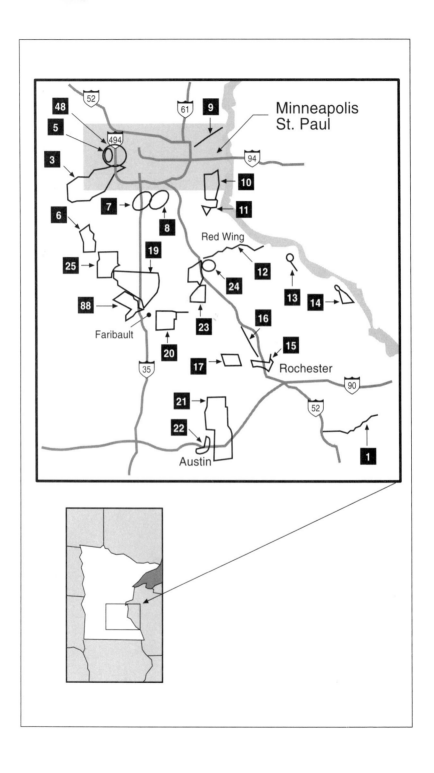

Contents

Introduction

The Land and its People

The Twin Cities and southeastern Minnesota offer the cyclist a rich variety of contrasts. One finds open expanse, even solitude, in rural areas. One finds densely populated urban settings with skyscrapers and heavy vehicular traffic. And one finds everything in between. The land was once the homeland for two Native American tribes, the Sioux and the Chippewa. Descendants of those clans live today in reservations near two tours included here, Shakopee (Tour 3) and Red Wing (Tour 12).

Now the land is populated by the descendants of native-born pioneers and by immigrants from every continent and their descendants. Today most of the early patterns of settlement on the land have been blurred by the process of intermarriage, physical mobility, and economic opportunity. One way to see these changes is by riding these trails; I have attempted throughout to point to the most important of these changes as they unfold in a variety of forms.

Along with the land, you will meet the people. Almost all of us have been characterized—properly, I believe—as being "Minnesota nice." William Swanson, in the October 1997 issue of *Mpls. St. Paul* magazine, defines this as "that famous combination of personal pleasantness, civic courtesy, and public decorum that so many of us believe have set us apart from the rude and rowdy world."

That means Minnesotans are friendly and cheerful, yet reserved. It means they are proud of their homes and towns but do little overt boasting about them. Minnesotans have a strong sense of geographic place and cultural heritage, and are happy to compare the special qualities of their towns favorably with those of their neighbors. As you ride, be sure to ask the local people you meet for more details about their communities and their histories. Most of the "Minnesota nice" people will gladly

9

reply. They will also often tell you about other worthwhile destinations to which you can ride.

This book thus offers two of the three ingredients you need for successful riding—land and people. The third, of course, is equipment.

Equipment

The Machine

You start with the purchase of a bicycle. Being open to a wide range of experiences, you decide on a machine somewhere on the spectrum from low-cost, pre-owned cycles to those breathtakingly expensive marvels. Some riders happily stay at the low end throughout their riding years; others just as happily progress upward as their riding skills and their leisure-time priorities become more focused.

I recommend that you find a dealer who will let you take a long test ride. Talk with friends and dealers, and don't (as I had to learn) be intimidated by those who talk technical jargon at the expense of down-to-earth advice. If the traditional touring/racing bicycle with its light weight and high gears is not attractive (although for many it is the only way to go), then explore the growing world of mountain bikes, which have the advantage of an upright riding position and more forgiving tires. My strongest advice: Given the enormous variety of colors, styles, components, and prices available, look on the purchase of a bicycle as a great learning experience. The alliance of rider and machine is a lifelong educational opportunity; with time, you will come to have an intimate relationship with your machine. Certain aspects of bicycle technology require the user to adjust to the bicycle, not the other way around. But the bicycle in some ways is like a riding horse; on its terms, it wants to please.

Gear

A good helmet is absolutely essential. Always wear it, even if it's only to take a spin on your driveway to test air pressure. (I erred here once, and am lucky that the helmetless spill didn't injure me.) A handlebar or saddle-seat storage bag is useful. So, too, is a water-bottle holder (or two) mounted on the frame. Spouse Ruth showed me the advantage of putting some ice cubes in the bottle before starting; cold water after a couple of hours of riding is a nice treat.

©MINNESOTA OFFICE OF TOURISM

On the road again

Also, always carry a sturdy lock and chain or other security device. Some riders prefer the U-locks; others choose the 3- to 4-foot chain locks with padlocks (key or combination). Note: Bicycles are very hot property for thieves or mischievous, joyriding pranksters. Always keep yours locked and secure when you aren't riding. For those who doubt, talk with bicycle shop dealers about "chop shops"—those places where stolen machines are skillfully dismantled, the basic parts mixed around, and reconfigured bicycles are put on sale.

When out of town, always carry personal identification, a credit card, and spare quarters for the telephone. The weather will dictate what extra clothing you will need: windbreakers, rain gear, head cover, and extra togs. Some riders bring along a compact notebook with pencil to preserve memories; a camera should be on your checklist too. Look also at the compact first-aid kits, which include adhesive bandages, gauze pads, moleskin, and sunscreen lotion.

Tools

Here is a test of your personality. The optimist says that no serious mishap will occur, so why take on extra weight and bulk with tools? The realist says that one never knows about such things, and will find room for items such as tire irons, a tube repair kit, a chain-link remover, a spoke wrench, and six spare spokes. The realist will also bring along a set of Allen wrenches, a tire pump that fastens on the bicycle frame, a Phillips screwdriver, and an adjustable wrench. Both agree that a rear-view mirror attached either to your helmet or to the handlebars is necessary. A map holder is also helpful; several styles are available, including those that attach to handlebar storage bags. And although you'll find one or more bicycle repair shops listed at the end of each tour, keep in mind that some of these may not be open depending on what time of day or day of the week you ride. Bicycle repair shops also have a remarkable way of opening and closing without very much warning, so call ahead.

To avoid saddle sores, purchase a gel-filled saddle or a sheepskin seat cover. Other gear items you should bring are padded cycling gloves, a compass, a flashlight, and heavy sheet plastic. Finally, I never go anywhere without my many-splendored Swiss Army knife.

Today a variety of low-priced, reliable cyclocomputers are available to provide information about speed, distance, time in motion, and related items. Depending on how successfully you mount one of these tiny

The bluff country of southeastern Minnesota was made for bicycling.

computers on your bike, they are not always models of uniform precision. So be generous if you find that your tenths-of-a-mile measurements are not exactly the same as mine! Also, when you ride around a park or similar facility in one of the side trips described in these tours, remember that the extra excursion will add to your total mileage, something I didn't factor in when measuring the mileage given in each tour.

Off and Pedaling

Before you set out, follow this checklist:
- Test the tire pressure, and inflate or deflate accordingly to match the recommended psi (pounds per square inch) for your bike; this information is usually imprinted on the side of each tire. Remember, low tires require you to exert a lot of extra energy that would be better spent in other ways.
- Spin each wheel freely to make sure the brake pads aren't rubbing.
- Check the quick-release levers at each wheel hub to make sure they are tight.

- Test the brakes.
- If you are going to ride at night, be sure the light(s) are working.
- Before you start one of these tours, have your machine registered with the local bureau of vehicle registration. This helps ensure a speedy recovery or insurance compensation if your bicycle is stolen.

Remember, the bicycle is considered a vehicle, meaning that you have both responsibilities and rights as its rider. Your responsibilities include using hand signals when turning or changing direction in traffic; obeying all road signs and traffic signals; always riding on the right side of traffic; and at night, always riding with lights: you must have a working red light mounted on the back of your bicycle, and a white light in front.

Ride in a straight line; pass on the left of slower bikes. A must: when you want to pass a slower cyclist in front of you, always warn them well in advance by saying "Passing on your left." Many cyclists disregard the six-sided red STOP sign and ride on through when no other vehicles are nearby. That is a violation of the law, and riders are just as subject to prosecution as are motor vehicle operators.

Finally, when you have to stop, always move off the road (whether it be an off-road trail or a regular highway). Don't take away any space from those coming after you. Lots of bumps, collisions, and angry tempers (not to say contusions and abrasions) will be avoided by this courtesy.

On the Road

Experts agree that most cyclists pedal much too slowly and in too high a gear. So gear down to make it easier to pedal, and try to increase your cadence up to 70 or 80 pedal revolutions per minute. My two fellow riders, to whom this book is dedicated, remind me of this very often!

Socializing when riding is one of this sport's greatest rewards; side-by-side talk will flow freely. But remember that in heavy traffic it is prudent to ride single file. Ride defensively; don't expect oncoming or trailing automobiles to see you even dimly; they are looking for other motorized vehicles. When you have no shoulder, leave yourself room—perhaps 3 feet—of margin. When rainy conditions prevail, be ready to brake more carefully and more often than you would in dry road situations. On downhills, keep more distance between riders than you do on

Lake Pepin, a part of the Mississippi River near Lake City

flat terrain. Apply your brakes sparingly: apply and release, apply and release. Give any hotdog cyclist all the space you think will guarantee your safety from his or her shenanigans. And another must: do not use portable radio headsets. Your ears, along with your eyes, are your best safety protection. Look at it this way: In addition to being alert to the presence of other vehicles on the road, you'll also be able to hear the sounds of birds, critters, and the wind. That is one of the real joys of on-road, right-in-the-middle-of-reality riding.

Remember, too, that you are just as entitled to the road as the driver of an automobile. In theory, that means you have the right to your strip of pavement; in practice, however, prudence suggests that when traffic backs up, you should pull over to the right. One rider has written that you should "use your brain rather than the universal salute when a driver does you wrong." When that happens, memorize the license plate and report the reckless driver to the police. Perhaps the officials will not follow up right away, but a frequently reported car and driver will eventually get their attention.

Left turns can be a challenge. You can negotiate those by signaling, then moving into the left lane and pedaling accordingly. Or you can ride straight through the intersection, dismount, and walk your machine across the street. The latter method is better at busy intersections.

Whew! With all those things to remember, can bicycling still be a fulfilling experience? Yes it can. You are in control and can tailor each cycling trip to your interests. That would include taking in lots of quality stops along the way: find antiques stores or eateries, or enjoy pleasant vistas from the brows of hills. For refreshment and renewal, nothing else is like it.

Sources of Information

This book offers tested information and advice on these 25 rides. Bicycling is rewarding, as I've said, because it is so much a self-creating experience. You have the freedom and flexibility to make your own trails, to break loose spontaneously from the planned tour. To help you plan your own itineraries, here are some basic sources of information. A fee is charged for some materials as noted; the rest are free.

Rather than trying to offer information on specific eateries or lodging, we include below some sources from which you can obtain this information to suit your own budget and preferences. In addition, be sure to check the bulletin boards that can be found at many bicycle stores; they usually feature cycling newsletters, information on group rides, bikes for sale, scrawled notes on 3x5 cards, and other useful information, some of which may surprise you!

Resources

For southeast Minnesota and the Twin Cities, these offices provide helpful, current information. Those who answer the telephones are cheerful and encouraging.

For statewide bicycling information, call the **State Bicycling Coordinator**, 612-297-1838.

The **Minnesota Department of Transportation** has a series of six maps covering the entire state. For an update on availability, call 612-296-2216 or 1-800-657-3757. Fee.

For the **Minneapolis Parks and Recreation Board**, call 612-661-4875.

For the **St. Paul Parks and Recreation Board**, call 612-266-6400.

For overall travel planning advice, call the **Minnesota Travel**

Information Center at 612-296-5029 or 1-800-657-3700 (this includes eateries and lodging).

For **Minnesota Bikeway maps**, call the Minnesota Bookstore at 612-297-3000 or 1-800-657-3757. Fee.

For a brochure on bicycle safety, call the **Minnesota Department of Public Safety**, 612-296-6652.

For information on all aspects of recreation in southeastern Minnesota, an indispensable source is the **Southern Regional Office, Minnesota Office of Tourism**, PO Box 286, Mankato 56001; 507-389-6258.

The **Twin Cities Bike Club** has a state bicycle atlas for sale; call 612-924-2443.

For club-sponsored day and weekend rides, call **American Youth Hostels**, 612-378-3773; or write to them at 125 SE Main Street, Suite 235, Minneapolis 55414.

Cities with Useful Information

The cities and towns on these tours have helpful sources of information for your rides. These are free for the asking.

Austin Convention and Visitors Bureau, 1301 18th Avenue NW, Austin 55912; 507-437-4563 or 1-800-444-5713.

Cannon Falls Chamber of Commerce, PO Box 2TD, 103 N. Fourth Street, Cannon Falls 55509; 507-263-2289, ext. 2.

Faribault Chamber of Commerce, PO Box 434, 530 Wilson Avenue, Faribault 55021; 507-334-4381 or 1-800-658-2354; fax: 507-334-1003.

Fountain Tourism, PO Box 115, Fountain 55935; 507-268-4449.

Harmony Tourism Center, PO Box 141, Harmony 55939; 1-800-246-MINN.

Hastings Chamber of Commerce, 1304 Vermillion Street, Hastings 55033; 507-894-4990.

Historic Bluff Country, PO Box 609, Harmony 55939; 507-886-2230; fax: 507-886-2818.

Jordan Chamber of Commerce, 315 Broadway South, Jordan 55352; 612-370-9141.

Kenyon Chamber of Commerce, 511 Second Street, Kenyon 55946; 507-789-6415.

Lake City Chamber of Commerce, 2212 Washington Street, PO Box 150, Lake City 55041; 1-800-368-4123; fax: 612-345-4123.

Lanesboro Office of Tourism, PO Box 20, Lanesboro 55949; 507-467-2696 or 1-800-994-2670; fax: 507-467-2468.

Mantorville Chamber of Commerce, PO Box 188, Mantorville 55955; 507-635-5170.

Montgomery Chamber of Commerce, PO Box 46, Montgomery 55069; 612-364-7331.

New Prague Chamber of Commerce, PO Box 191, New Prague 55071; 612-758-4360.

Northfield Chamber of Commerce, PO Box 198, 500 Water Street, Northfield 55057; 507-645-5604 or 1-800-658-2548; fax: 507-663-7782.

Red Wing Convention and Visitors Bureau, 418 Levee Street, Red Wing 55066; 612-385-5934 or 1-800-498-3444; fax: 612-388-6991.

Rochester Convention and Visitors Bureau, 150 South Broadway, Rochester 55904; 507-288-4331 or 1-800-634-8277; fax: 507-288-9144.

Rushford Tourism Information: *See* Historic Bluff Country, above.

Wabasha Chamber of Commerce, 257 West Main Sreet, PO Box 105, Wabasha 55981; 612-565-4158 or 1-800-565-4158; fax: 612-565-4541.

A Few Definitions

Trail: those rides where the route is free (except for intersection crossings) of any motorized traffic.
Tour: one specific ride.
Path: In Minnesota the word "path" is rarely used regarding bicycle riding. Here, a bicycle path is called a "trail."

PART ONE:
TWO CLASSIC TRAILS

Two Classic Trails

I've chosen to start this guide with two of the best-known bicycle trails in Minnesota.

The Root River Trail in the historic bluff country of southeastern Minnesota embraces some of the most astonishing and rewarding scenery in all of America. Its rural isolation, village charm, and river-hugging roadbeds are not to be missed. The trail managers keep adding spurs to its main line; in 1996 five miles of new trail were added, extending east beyond the village of Rushford.

The Cannon Valley Trail has its own charms, not the least of which is its isolation. The trail follows the Cannon River on a flat to gently rolling roadbed with the surrounding countryside teeming with wildlife, flowers, and birds. Both rides are directly accessible from major highways.

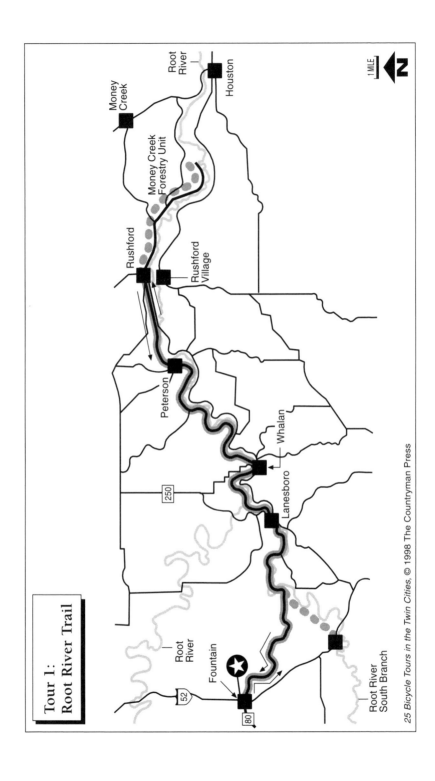

Tour 1:
Root River Trail

Money Creek

Root River

Houston

Money Creek Forestry Unit

Rushford

Rushford Village

Peterson

Whalan

Lanesboro

250

Root River

Fountain

52

80

Root River South Branch

1 MILE

N

25 Bicycle Tours in the Twin Cities, © 1998 The Countryman Press

1

Root River Trail

Distance: *59 miles round-trip*
Terrain: *Flat to moderately rolling, one long hill; active but not crowded bike-path traffic*
Location: *Fillmore and Houston Counties*
Special features: *Scenery, five villages, fresh pies*

The Root River Trail is ideal for riders of all ages because clear options as to length are available on any segment of the ride. The basic trail goes from Fountain to Rushford, with new spurs being developed frequently. Built on an abandoned railroad grade, the round-trip is 59 miles, with several easy-on and easy-off accesses for shorter rides.

The trail is enhanced by the services of five villages along its course, each with its own personality. You are likely to see plenty of wildlife—migrating geese, wild turkeys, buzzards, songbirds, bald eagles, and deer. Campgrounds are available for overnight stays, as are a variety of B&Bs. The trail also passes picnic grounds and food stores.

The distinctive limestone bluffs along the Root River were sculpted by the interplay of water and wind. The bluffs create a cathedral effect; be sure to note their many splendid vistas as you ride through them on this trail.

This ride begins at the well-marked parking lot in Fountain, 28 miles south of Rochester on US 52. From US 52 turn east onto CR 8, and find the large parking lot and information kiosk. Just before you arrive at the lot, you'll see the Fillmore County Historic Center, which features a fine collection of reconstructed buildings depicting the area's traditions. Take a look around before you start the actual ride. In Fountain, note the bicycle painted on the city water tower; this is bicycle country!

A bridge and bluff over the Root River

0.0   *Head east and be prepared for a gradual but steady descent.*
You are cycling past a grainfield and will go by a graveyard (for other cemeteries, see Tours 23 and 24).

4.5   *Cross the first bridge, over Watson Creek.*

6.5   *Find the turnoff to the right (south) to Preston.*
This could be an additional ride, at another time. It's a 10-mile round-trip on a newly surfaced roadbed. Today, stay on the main trail.

6.7   *See the remarkable rock features created by blasting during railroad construction.*

6.9   *Pass the trail's campground, Old Barn Resort.*

7.0   *Ride over a great iron bridge, in excellent repair.*

9.5   *Note the soaring cliffs ahead of you, just before Lanesboro.*

11.1   *Enter Lanesboro.*
All of downtown Lanesboro is on the National Register of Historic Places. The town has superb restaurants, museums, shops, inns,

and fun places such as a tattoo parlor and the Sons of Norway lodge. The Minnesota State Department of Natural Resources Depot, right on the trail, can supply you with information on the ride, side trips, and accommodations. You'll also find water and rest rooms there.

This town was dying before the trail came; now it thrives.

13.1 Head east to Whalan.

Here the bluffs are in full view, again creating the cathedral-like effect.

14.5 Enter Whalan, and note the Overland Inn right on the trail.

Stop here for one of the inn's many flavors of pies, fresh-baked daily. A Scandinavian gift shop is nearby.

14.8 Keep heading east, watching for whitewater along the river.

20.0 Notice the spiffy farm.

24.5 Enter Peterson.

This town has a nice city park, food and water, supplies, antiques stores, and lodging. A kiosk explains Peterson's history.

27.5 For the next mile enjoy one final spectacular scenic vista.

29.5 Enter Rushford.

Here you'll find bike shops offering equipment and repair services, as well as soda pop, ice cream, ATMs, telephones, pleasant restaurants, and lodging. The latest addition to the trail, known as Money Creek Forestry Unit, stretches for 5.8 miles eastward. More extensions are planned in 1998.

29.5 Now it's time to turn around and double your riding pleasure by riding back to Fountain.

Bicycle Repair Service

Little River General Store, 104 & 106 Parkway Avenue North, Lanesboro, 507-467-2943 or 1-800-994-2943

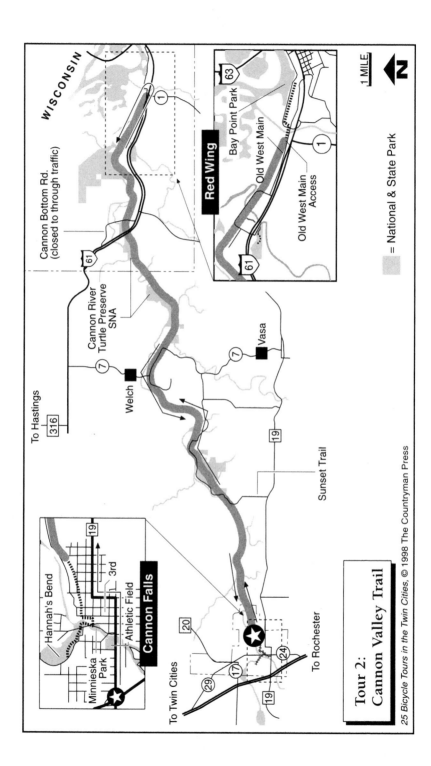

WISCONSIN

Cannon Bottom Rd.
(closed to through traffic)

① 61

Cannon River
Turtle Preserve
SNA

To Hastings

316

⑦

Welch

Vasa

⑦

19

Sunset Trail

Red Wing

63

Bay Point Park

Old West Main

Old West Main
Access

① 1

61

1 MILE

N

= National & State Park

Cannon Falls

19

3rd

Hannah's Bend

Athletic Field

Minnieska
Park

To Twin Cities

20

29

17

19

24

To Rochester

**Tour 2:
Cannon Valley Trail**

25 Bicycle Tours in the Twin Cities, © 1998 The Countryman Press

2

Cannon Valley Trail

Distance: *39.4 miles*
Terrain: *Flat to very gentle rises; busy bike-trail traffic on weekends; also used by joggers and in-line skaters*
Location: *Goodhue County*
Special features: *Wildlife, flowers, interpretive signboards*

This trail is privately owned and managed and offers a variety of treats. Almost totally isolated from towns, it meanders through an area rich with wildlife, flowers, and birds. The gentle Cannon River flows alongside most of the way, eventually running into the Mississippi River. At a number of stops you'll find picnic benches, rest rooms, drinking water, and explanations of the area's ecology and history. Cannon Valley features serenity, and mostly flat terrain on its paved-over railroad bed. If you're looking for a few hours of relaxing exercise on your favorite machine, this is the tour for you.

The trail starts in downtown Cannon Falls (see also Tours 23 and 24) at the parking lot where MN 19, MN 20, and CR 24 join. The parking lot is 0.5 mile east of US 52, the Cannon Falls exit, or 200 yards west of the only traffic light in downtown Cannon Falls. The Cannon Valley Trail charges a fee of $2 per day for riders 18 and over; $10 for a season pass.

0.0 *Start at the information board, where you can read descriptions of what to see.*

0.1 *You drop quickly along the waterfall here, where the Cannon "falls."*

Note the charming city park and flower garden. Watch for the stunning wildflowers along the entire trail; something is always in bloom, including daisies, sunflowers, brown-eyed Susans, and day lilies.

A Cannon Valley Trail paradise

2.8   *Pause here for a great view.*

The trail hugs the limestone rock cut out for the railroad, and has on the left a marvelous view of this gentle valley. On your right are abundant flowers growing out of the rocks. Be ready to spot wild turkey, woodchucks, and deer.

3.8   *Find the Anderson Memorial Rest Area.*

This is a good place for a picnic, especially for younger riders, who by now are probably ready for a pause, even with the downhill terrain. Rest rooms and picnic tables are here, and there is a walking path to the river.

5.6   *On your left is the land the State of Minnesota has designated the "River Terrace Prairie."*

Dismount and walk up the embankment to view the abundant vegetation.

6.1   *Stop at the Trail Interpretive Center board and display.*

Here is a clear explanation of the valley's ecosystem. Watch for colorful birds flying through, such as the scarlet tanager, indigo bunting, and Baltimore oriole.

6.6 *Note on the left the great dairy and grain farm, making full use of the rich soil, abundant water, and shelter of the valley.*

9.5 *Pass a private campground, Hidden Valley.*

On weekends the variety of tents pitched here is a sight to see. In summer the camp also attracts season-long RV residents.

10.0 *Enter Welch and find the beautifully kept Trail Station.*

Here you have fresh water, picnic tables, rest rooms, a telephone, and, on the bulletin boards, helpful information on local wildlife. The village of Welch is 0.3 miles to the north on CR 7; it has a coffeehouse and some Cannon Valley memorabilia.

11.4 *Cross the long, bumpy bridge over Belle Creek.*

During the floods of 1993 and 1997, this structure was inundated. From here to Red Wing, the trail is more enclosed with foliage.

13.4 *Here is the Cannon River Turtle Preserve, protected as a State Natural Area.*

15.0 *You pass under US 61.*

Find a tidy rest area with benches and bike stands. Ahead is the railroad flycatcher built to warn crew members (or freeloaders) of the oncoming low bridge.

16.1 *You arrive at the Red Wing Archaeological Preserve.*

Park your bike and walk the 100 yards to its interpretive center. The preserve documents evidence of Native American dwellings on this site dating back several hundred years. You'll see remains of storage pits, fortifications, and burial grounds.

17.2 *View on the left the former beaver dam plain, which ran for several miles.*

The 1993 flood drove the beavers away, but most of the dam remains.

19.0 *On your right you'll see the turnoff to A.P. Anderson Park.*

Riding on, going east, note at Tyler Road the Tom Thumb store, which sells fresh marshmallow Rice Krispie treats. It also has an air pump for your tires.

19.4 *Arrive at the other end of the trail, at Bench Street (CR 1).*

You are now inside Red Wing city limits. Rest awhile, turn around, and head back to Cannon Falls. Happy trails!

Bicycle Repair Service

Trail Station Sports, 106 Fourth Street North, Cannon Falls; 507-263-5055 or 1-888-835-BIKE

PART TWO:
THE TWIN CITIES

A Biker's Smorgasbord

The Twin Cities and environs offer a delightful array of rides. There are city lakes and croplands, mighty rivers and shaded parks, shopping malls and hilltop vistas. You could spend a rewarding summer cycling around the Seven County Metro area, this being the standard definition of the area's boundary lines.

Diversity is one element in the smorgasbord; accessibility is a second. The huge increase in recreational biking in the past 20 years has convinced city planners of the benefits of providing interesting, safe, and well-maintained bike routes. In the Twin Cities, most of the long-range planning has been completed; now surrounding cities and towns are implementing those plans and adding their own routes. The casual as well as the dedicated cyclist can find rewarding rides within a few miles or less from home.

For all of this variety, however, a certain unity is present. The use of the routes reflects a way of life that takes full advantage of the good weather in the five or six months that riding is available. Memories of zero-degree weather and howling blizzards create a kind of urgency that keeps riders on these trails in good weather. Unity flourishes also among riders, from new friendships made and existing ones strengthened through the camaraderie of the trails. Many riders form informal clubs, such as the Wednesday Wanderers and the professional Gopher Wheelmen. Just wear a commemorative T-shirt from an organized ride and someone will start a conversation with you about it. Bicycle shops serve as convenient centers for many riders. Talk flows easily when kindred spirits discuss equipment, favorite trails, or plans for the next ride. Together the many bikers using these eight trails find fresh ways to enjoy their remarkable machines.

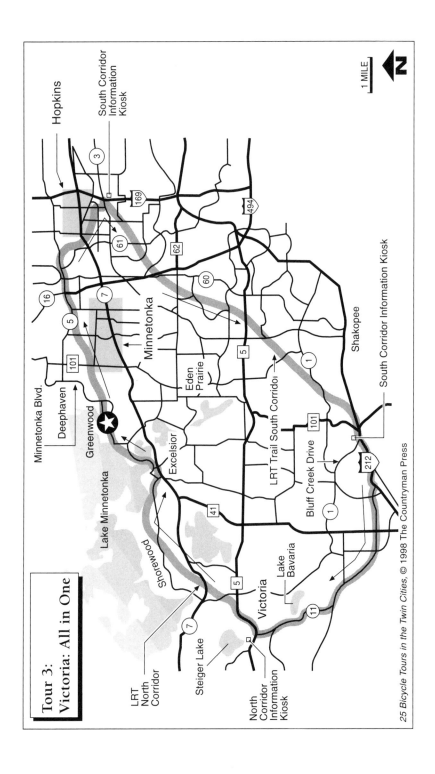

Tour 3:
Victoria: All in One

Hopkins

South Corridor
Information
Kiosk

Minnetonka Blvd.

Deephaven

Greenwood

Lake Minnetonka

Shorewood

Steiger Lake

LRT
North
Corridor

North
Corridor
Information
Kiosk

Victoria

Lake
Bavaria

Minnetonka

Eden
Prairie

Excelsior

LRT Trail South Corridor

Bluff Creek Drive

Shakopee

South Corridor Information Kiosk

1 MILE

N

25 Bicycle Tours in the Twin Cities, © 1998 The Countryman Press

3

Victoria: All in One

Distance: *36.5 miles*
Terrain: *Flat to rolling countryside; active suburban traffic on open rural roads; about half the ride is on bike trails*
Location: *Hennepin and Carver Counties*
Special features: *Lake Minnetonka, five golf courses, small-town ambience, great vistas*

This is one of the most diverse tours in this book. It is the only one with crushed rock in the roadbed; this lasts for just under half the mileage. Within a few minutes you will find the surface easily manageable. This ride is, in fact, two trails plus a rural connecting road. The Hennepin County Park Board calls these trails the North Corridor and the South Corridor, with connections at Hopkins and Victoria. The whole facility is known as the Southwest Regional LRT ("light rail transit") Trail.

To park, take exit 17 west from I-494 and go on MN 5 for 4.1 miles to Deephaven. Find the trail depot, at Cottagewood Grove Avenue. Park there, and note the information kiosk.

The trail you are on parallels Minnetonka Boulevard, a major artery to downtown Minneapolis.

0.0 *Starting at the depot, head east.*

1.2 *Pass a public golf course.*

You are very close to one of Minnesota's great treasures, Lake Minnetonka, which you will see up close later. The bird life is abundant in this area.

1.7 *Note the stop light at MN 101, one of several on this leg.*

3.7 *City Hall is on your left.*

J.D. Hanson views a golf course, his natural habitat.

4.1   *You ride under I-494.*

Note Minnehaha Creek, which flows through Minneapolis (you ride alongside the creek on Tour 4).

4.8   *Note St. David's Episcopal Church, a local landmark.*

You are in a bustling commercial district, but the trail avoids any motorized traffic except at the crossings.

6.6   *Enter Hopkins, the "raspberry capital" of America.*

Find some berries in season. If you're here in summer, enjoy the annual celebration.

7.0   *The North Corridor trail ends; find the kiosk and note the directions. Turn right (south) on Eighth Avenue S.*

7.4   *The South Corridor information kiosk here has tables and parking. Turn right (west) and you are on the second part of this trail.*

9.7 *Ride under I-494 again.*

10.5 *Note the blacktop surface here as you ride over MN 62, also known as the Crosstown. Follow the directions painted on the trail as* LRT.

10.7 *Cross the railroad track and continue to ride westward following the sharp, clearly marked turn.*

11.8 *Pass Edenvale Golf Course and Edenvale Park.*

12.7 *Be ready for a short, stiff hill; you may want to walk it.*

13.0 *See the private Bent Creek golf course on your left.*

14.8 *Cross over Eden Prairie Road and enter the city of Eden Prairie.*

15.2 *Find the fourth golf course, Bearpath.*

Jack Nicklaus designed this course especially for this gated community, which is one of the many upscale residential areas built on golf courses in the 1990s. Look north to see Lake Riley Park.

18.1 *Be ready for a tour highlight, a wonderful scenic overlook of the Minnesota River Valley.*

Here are the grain elevators—some of America's largest, such as Cargill and Archer-Daniel-Midlands; note the grain barges. The city you see is Shakopee, with its great stone church.

18.8 *You cross over MN 101, a rather steep section.*

19.5 *The South Corridor Trail formally ends here at the information kiosk. You are now at Bluff Creek Drive, with parking. Informally, the trail continues west for another mile; continue riding on it.*

20.5 *Turn right onto US 212, heading west.*

You now will be riding alongside motorized traffic, but this is a fine lane for bicycles. Look for the Super 8 Motel sign for a direction check. This is a very short lap.

20.9 *Turn right onto CR 11, also known as Engler Boulevard.*

Stay on Engler Boulevard for several miles, noting that it eventually turns into Victoria Drive. Some uphill riding starts here;

the shoulders are wide and the road is clearly marked. Note the entrance sign to the town of Chaska, founded in 1851, and home of two U.S. Open National Golf Championship Tournaments (at Hazeltine National Golf Club).

22.4 Park Ridge, a community crossroads, is on the right; continue north on CR 11.

This is the public center of Chaska. Find a walking/bicycle path just on the right. As you ride on this path you pass through totally rural croplands, with corn, forage, and soybeans. Note the well-kept farm buildings throughout.

24.9 Towering Harvestore silos dominate your view.

25.7 You're at Lake Bavaria.

You go up a long hill here, gentle and winding.

26.5 Enter Victoria, the westernmost of the villages, and clearly not a suburb.

26.8 Pass the fifth golf course, Victoria, and a great Catholic church with manicured grounds.

27.6 Cross MN 5, continuing on CR 11.

28.5 Find the west end start of the North Corridor Trail at the information kiosk at Stieger Lake.

You might want to look around Victoria, which has food, drinking water, and telephones. You are back on crushed rock; expect some bumps from here on.

32.7 Enter the town of Shorewood, and approach Lake Minnetonka.

Here are several wonderful views of the bays.

33.6 Enter Excelsior.

This is a carefully planned restoration town with specialty shops, restricted traffic flow, spectacular mural art on buildings, and genuine small-town charm.

34.4 Find marinas galore here.

This is a major recreation area. Note everywhere the beautiful homes.

35.9 You're back in Deephaven.

36.5 *You return to your car; the all-in-one smorgasbord ride is complete.*

Bicycle Repair Services

Now Sports, 426 Main Street, Hopkins, 612-935-8207

Area Wide Cycles, 229 Water Street, Excelsior, 612-474-3229

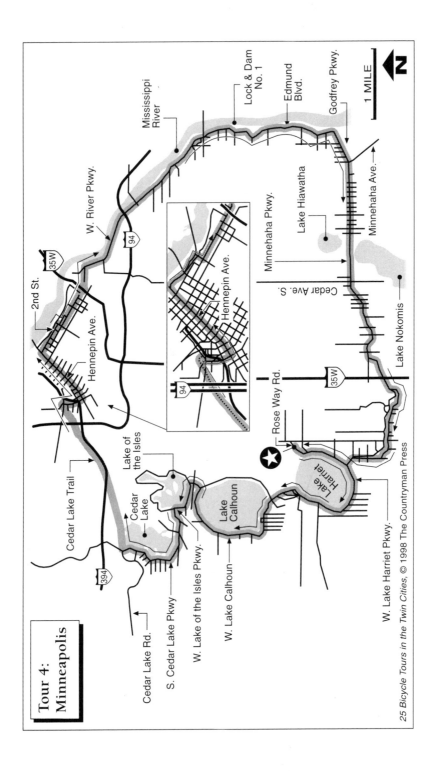

Tour 4:
Minneapolis

Mississippi River

Lock & Dam No. 1

Edmund Blvd.

Godfrey Pkwy.

1 MILE

W. River Pkwy.

94

35W

2nd St.

Hennepin Ave.

Hennepin Ave.

94

Minnehaha Pkwy.

Lake Hiawatha

Minnehaha Ave.

Cedar Ave. S.

Lake Nokomis

Rose Way Rd.

35W

Lake Harriet

Cedar Lake Trail

Lake of the Isles

Cedar Lake

Lake Calhoun

394

Cedar Lake Rd.

S. Cedar Lake Pkwy

W. Lake of the Isles Pkwy.

W. Lake Calhoun

W. Lake Harriet Pkwy.

25 Bicycle Tours in the Twin Cities, © 1998 The Countryman Press

4

Minneapolis

Distance: 26.2 miles
Terrain: Flat to moderately hilly; includes downtown urban traffic and
several quiet bicycle trails
Location: Hennepin County
Special features: Lakes, downtown, the Mississippi, the West River
Parkway, Minnehaha Parkway Trail

Minneapolis is remarkable for having a huge variety of neighborhoods contained in a rather small area. This tour goes into many of them, in quick succession. You'll see lakes, stunning homes, commercial and industrial warehouse areas, the university, the entertainment district, a Federal Reserve Bank, Pillsbury's mill, hospitals, elegant riverside walks, Old Man River, Lock and Dam No. 1 (see Tour 11 for No. 2), lots of noble oak trees, and a trans-city parkway. The bike routes also provide ample water, picnic tables, and rest rooms.

Amazingly, this twin city is still much like a town—easy to enter, easy to leave, and protective of its history while improving its recreational facilities, such as biking trails.

Park at the Lake Harriet Rose Garden location, on Rose Way Road off East Lake Harriet Parkway. To get there, take I-35W to 46th Street, go west on 46th Street to East Lake Harriet Parkway. Turn right (north) onto Rose Way Road, and find the Rose Garden lot on your left. A fee of $1 per day is charged.

You will start at the same point in Tour 5, and ride part of the Four Lakes Loop. Besides biking, you can in-line skate, walk, jog, swim, fish, windsurf, sail, and canoe. The architecture is a feast of immaculate homes and mansions with well-groomed lawns, original trees, and great views. You may want to dismount to take it all in.

0.0   Head toward the lake and turn left (south) onto East Lake Harriet Parkway.

Note that the bicycle traffic moves only clockwise here, and that pedestrians have a separate trail. Be advised that on occasion the bicycle trails become two-way traffic; these changes are clearly marked.

0.8   Find a wonderful old water pump with great-tasting water.

2.3   You come to a stoplight at the intersection of East Lake Harriet Parkway and 42nd Street.

Here you'll find a major community center: the Lake Harriet Bandshell, a nearby refectory, rest rooms, picnic grounds, and a restored city streetcar now in use for a short run. This is Minneapolis at its best.

2.6   Turn left (northwest) onto William Berry Parkway.

2.8   You arrive at West Lake Calhoun Parkway, and the second of the four lakes. Turn left (west) and ride clockwise around Lake Calhoun.

This area features lovely homes and handsome, gold-domed St. Mary's Greek Orthodox Church.

5.0   Arrive at the cloverleaf, which takes you to Lake of the Isles.

You'll find a concession stand, water, and rest rooms here.

5.3   Follow the signs through the cloverleaf, down and under the street and you will come to West Lake of the Isles Parkway. Ride west on it, clockwise around the lake.

5.8   You'll find an information map here.

6.0   At the bridge, turn left (west) onto Dean Parkway.

6.3   Turn right (northwest) onto South Cedar Lake Parkway, taking you to Cedar Lake, the fourth lake on this loop.

7.5   Cross Cedar Lake Road at the stop light. See the sign for the Cedar Lake Trail (also known as the Ewing Trail), and continue on.

7.7   As you come to a major intersection, one bicycle trail goes left and the other turns right. Take the latter, the Ewing Trail, also known as the Cedar Lake Trail. Head downtown (east).

©MINNESOTA OFFICE OF TOURISM

The Minnehaha Parkway winds through Minneapolis

43

Note how quickly the setting changes. This is light industrial, commercial, railroad country. The huge building on your left is the International Market Square; note, too, the busy gravel pit.

10.3 You go uphill a bit here, just before the trail ends at 10.5 miles.

The trail ends at the intersection of 12th Street and Glenwood on the edge of downtown.

10.5 Turn right (west) and see 12th Street. Turn left (south) onto 12th Street and ride on it to Hennepin Avenue.

10.6 Arrive at the launching point, 12th Street and Hennepin Avenue. Turn left (east) onto Hennepin.

The bicycle trail is painted clearly on the street on your left. Follow the trail to the bridge some 10 blocks away.

You are now riding through the entertainment and shopping district of Minneapolis. You go near Target Center, the Minneapolis Public Library, the Federal Reserve Bank, and the famous Northwestern National Life Insurance building. Every intersection has a stop light, as you go from 10th Street to First Street.

11.7 Ride onto the right (or south) side of the Hennepin Avenue Suspension Bridge. (You'll only be on the bridge for a short distance.)

11.8 Turn right at the green sign for the St. Anthony Falls Heritage Trail, just a few feet onto the bridge. Ride down the trail in switchback fashion.

11.9 At the Mississippi, find the information map for local points of interest.

12.0 Head right (south) on the trail, alongside First Street South.

This is the heart of the old mill district, with many elevators and mills still intact. Note Pillsbury on your left.

12.3 Turn right (west) onto Portland Avenue South, at the sign for the bicycle trail, and ride two blocks to Second Street South. Turn left (south) onto Second Street South and ride six blocks.

Locate the sign directing you to the West River Parkway, your destination. See the famous Old Stone Bridge, one of the first in Minneapolis over the Mississippi.

12.5 *Follow the signs for Second Street South through the underpass (I-35W). Turn right (south) onto West River Parkway.*

You'll soon pass the University of Minnesota on your left. Ride past sandy beaches, the Fairview Medical Center, and a greenbelt. Take some time to enjoy the leisurely pace.

15.1 *You are riding on one of the city's most famous streets, the West River Parkway.*

You will be riding up some hefty hills, going through gorgeous neighborhoods. Keep following the bicycle trail signs as the road bends and curves. Continue riding on the left side of the road, headed south.

17.8 *Note that West River Parkway becomes Edmund Boulevard around East 34th Street*

18.3 *Arrive at the turnoff to Lock and Dam No. 1 and the Ford Bridge.*

Here is an interesting side trip, taking about an hour of riding and viewing. If you go here, you will ride alongside the Mississippi River, as in Tours 11–15. By now Edmund Boulevard has become Godfrey Parkway.

19.2 *Turn right (west) onto East Minnehaha Parkway. This is a wonderful greenbelt following a creek that goes through all of south Minneapolis, east to west, and out to Chaska (see Tour 3).*

20.1 *Find a fifth lake, Lake Nokomis, with a good bicycle riding trail around it (not included in this itinerary).*

A few years ago a fisherman caught a 44-pound northern pike in this lake! You can tell you are close (about 3 miles away) to the Twin City International Airport.

20.5 *Find an information kiosk, and cross Cedar Avenue (see Tour 8).*

Soon this road becomes West Minnehaha Parkway.

22.4 *On West Minnehaha Parkway, ride under I-35W.*

Find some rather sharp curves, bumpy surfaces, and crossovers from north to south as you go west.

24.5 *You return to Lake Harriet Parkway. Turn right (north) and proceed to the Rose Garden.*

26.2 You're back at your car. Now you've seen it all.

Bicycle Repair Services

Penn Cycle, 6824 Penn Avenue South, Minneapolis, 612-866-7540

All Brand Bicycle Repair, 2920 Lyndale Avenue South, Minneapolis, 612-825-8216

Erik's Bike Shop, 7144 Chicago Avenue South, Minneapolis, 612-861-3011

5

Four Lakes Loop

Distance: 12.4 miles; more if you circle the lakes more than once
Terrain: Flat; active traffic with people on foot and on wheels on parts
  of the trail
Location: Hennepin County
Special features: Lakes, homes, lawns, marinas

This is one of the shortest but most flexible of the tours in this book in
that you can easily lengthen it in several ways. Frank Lloyd Wright called
the Minneapolis lakes "the fair jewels of a beautiful city," and so they are.
Some of this ride overlaps with Tour 4, but the redundancy is rewarding.
Indeed, many cyclists on this loop insist that it's fun to ride it over and
over, around the lakes. (For more information, order the Minneapolis
Lake District Map from the Map Store; 612-227-6277.)

Four lakes—three connected by channels—make up this ride. The
total mileage around each lake is: Lake Harriet, 2.7; Lake Calhoun, 3.1;
Lake of the Isles, 2.7; and Cedar Lake (only a partial loop), 1.7 one way.
The mileage markers listed in the tour below are based on one complete
circuit of each lake; riding clockwise, you will ride part of the way
around each lake on the first leg of the tour, completing each clockwise
lake circuit on the second leg on your way back to your car. You may increase your mileage by circling any or all of the lakes more than once.

These lake paths are very clearly marked. Usually there are two
trails—one for people on wheels, the other for pedestrians. At times the
two trails merge, as marked. Watch also for signs as to when you ride
only one way, and when two-way traffic prevails. Picnic tables, rest
rooms, water, and other necessities are available. You usually ride only a
few feet from the water, something of a delight for younger cyclists, who
should thrive on the loop.

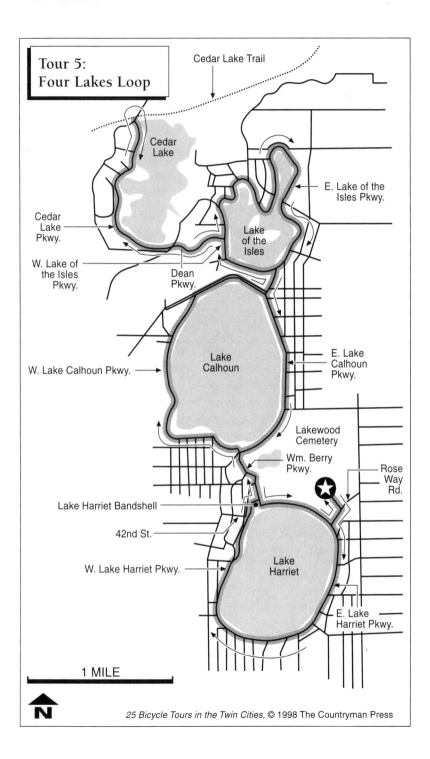

Tour 5:
Four Lakes Loop

Cedar Lake Trail

Cedar Lake

E. Lake of the Isles Pkwy.

Cedar Lake Pkwy.

W. Lake of the Isles Pkwy.

Lake of the Isles

Dean Pkwy.

Lake Calhoun

W. Lake Calhoun Pkwy.

E. Lake Calhoun Pkwy.

Lakewood Cemetery

Wm. Berry Pkwy.

Rose Way Rd.

Lake Harriet Bandshell

42nd St.

W. Lake Harriet Pkwy.

Lake Harriet

E. Lake Harriet Pkwy.

1 MILE

N

25 Bicycle Tours in the Twin Cities, © 1998 The Countryman Press

The Lake Harriet Bandshell

Besides just enjoying the ride, you'll have plenty to see: churches, historical sites, some restored Twin City streetcars now in summer service for excursions, concession stands, fishing docks, lovely trees and gardens, water sports, and specialty shops. And the people-watching is outstanding.

Park at the Lake Harriet Rose Garden location, on Rose Way Road off East Lake Harriet Parkway. To get there, take I-35W to 46th Street, turn west onto 46th Street, and go to East Lake Harriet Parkway. Turn right (north) onto Rose Way Road and find the Rose Garden lot on your left. A fee of $1 per day is charged. Or find a spot in the parking lots marked with the green P sign; most charge a nominal fee. Plan to arrive early; the lots are usually full by midmorning.

0.0 *From Rose Way Road, turn left (south) onto East Lake Harriet Parkway and ride clockwise around Lake Harriet.*

Look for the Lake Harriet bandshell, which presents free Sunday evening concerts; a refectory; a bird sanctuary; remodeled streetcars; and attractive homes.

2.3 *At the north end of Lake Harriet, turn left (north) onto the William Berry Parkway, which brings you to Lake Calhoun.*

To increase your mileage, you can continue riding all the way around Lake Harriet, and then return to this point to continue your tour.

2.7 *Turn left onto Lake Calhoun Parkway and ride clockwise around the lake.*

Lake Calhoun is surrounded by several marinas, and handsome craft ply its waters. One of my favorite buildings along this route is St. Mary's Greek Orthodox Church, topped by a gold dome. This lakeshore is also crowded with commercial and apartment buildings, and their residents also use the trails. Your path may be busy.

Again, you may circle the lake if you wish, or proceed directly to mile 4.6.

4.6 *For a side excursion, ride east on Lake Street at its junction with Lake Calhoun Parkway at the northeastern end of the lake.*

You'll arrive at Uptown, one of the Twin Cities' major specialty shopping centers (also known as Yuptown, for the yuppies who frequent it).

4.6 *Back at Lake Calhoun Parkway, follow the cloverleaf signs to Lake of the Isles. Ride around this lake clockwise on Lake of the Isles Parkway.*

Note its eye-pleasing blend of lake, lawns, and homes. Circle this lake more than once if you like, or proceed directly to mile 5.1

5.1 *At the southwestern corner of Lake of the Isles, take the Dean Parkway west to Cedar Lake.*

5.6 *Ride around the west side of Cedar Lake clockwise on the Cedar Lake Parkway for 1.2 miles, until you reach your turnaround point at the northwestern end of the lake.*

The trail does not loop Cedar Lake.

6.8 *At the northwestern corner of Cedar Lake, make a U-turn at the sign for Cedar Road. Finish the Four Lakes Loop by completing the loop around each lake until you arrive back at the Lake Harriet Rose Garden.*

12.4 You're back at the Lake Harriet Rose Garden and your car.
Why not do it again? Frank Lloyd Wright would understand.

Bicycle Repair Service

Calhoun Cycle, 1622 West Lake Street, Minneapolis, 612-827-8231

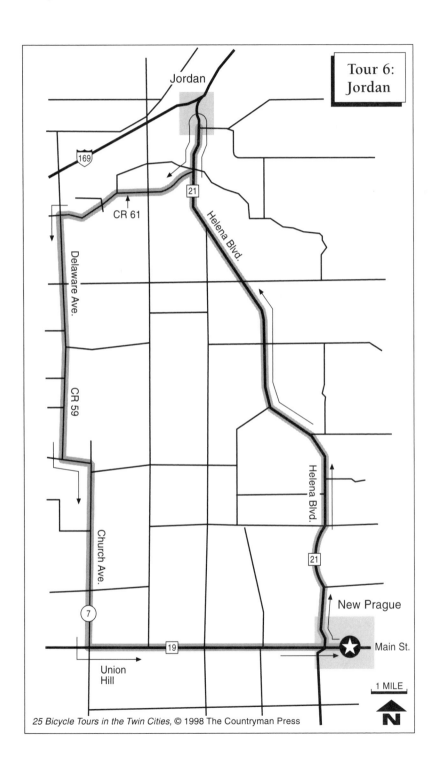

Tour 6:
Jordan

Jordan

169

CR 61

21

Helena Blvd.

Delaware Ave.

CR 59

Helena Blvd.

Church Ave.

21

New Prague

7

19

Main St.

Union
Hill

1 MILE

N

25 Bicycle Tours in the Twin Cities, © 1998 The Countryman Press

6

Jordan

Distance: *25.7 miles*
Terrain: *Flat to rolling countryside; low-density motor traffic*
Location: *Carver and Le Sueur Counties*
Special features: *Two stone churches, small-town ambience, quiet*

This ride defines the western border of the Twin Cities area as bounded by the Minnesota River. Jordan, the principal town, is home for commuters; its leaders actively seek to attract more businesses and residents. Yet one could live here with little daily contact with the other suburbs; it is a transition location. Jordan's ethnic heritage is more mixed than in many other communities nearby. Its people have stoutly resisted becoming an artsy-craftsy tourist destination, even though its lovely valley setting would certainly draw visitors. Jordan's schools are consolidated, it continues to support its traditional churches, and there are enough essential business services to keep it independent from the Wal-Marts and fast-food franchises. And the town is in the middle of excellent farmland, as productive as you will find in the entire region.

The tour starts in New Prague. To get there, drive south on I-35 to exit 69. Turn right (west) onto CR 2. Drive 7 miles, and turn left (south) onto CR 23. In 2 miles, turn west (right) onto CR 19, and drive the 6 miles to New Prague.

To park, find the lot next to Schumacher's. (This is also the start for Tour 25). It is on the corner of Main Street (MN 19) and Second Avenue SW.

0.0 *Turn left (west) out of the lot and look for MN 21, also known as Helena Boulevard.*

The road to Jordan beckons

0.1   Turn right (north) onto MN 21 and head toward Jordan.

Note the technology centers, on your right, that have kept agriculture thriving here: Farm Systems, Harvestore, and the like. This road has fine shoulders and some great views. The farms are far apart, suggesting that the pioneer homesteads are now extinct, their smaller landholdings unrealistic in today's world of agribusiness.

4.1   On the left, you'll see some yard art at a beautiful farm.

6.8   Pass by the elegant houses on this stretch.

Some of these are residences of Twin City commuters, most of them getaway retreats.

8.0   This sagging barn may remind you of how you feel after, say, a 50-mile ride.

9.0   You descend and come into Jordan, with its well-planned Wayside Park serving as the town's entryway.

Wayside is snuggled into a quiet valley; there are picnic tables and rest rooms, if you need to stop. See the creamery as evidence of the onetime bustling dairy business, now vanished due to high-tech dairy product trucks that transport milk to the large production centers.

9.6   Ride along the main street, Broadway.

Note the absence of tourist traps. Find St. John the Baptist Church, a highlight. This is a major regional landmark, beautifully preserved and with an active parochial school. I recommend that you stop to walk through and around the church.

9.7   Make a U-turn and go back on Broadway.

10.2   Turn right (southwest) onto CR 61.

13.4   Turn left (south) onto CR 59, also known as Delaware Avenue.

See St. Lawrence Town Hall. You are in some great farmland, on a recently resurfaced but seldom used road. This creates a wonderful sense of isolation from many of the other suburban communities.

16.4   Here is a showpiece dairy farm and home.

The farm is immaculate, with splendid trees, lawns, and outbuildings. It's worth taking a picture.

18.3   The road bends slightly to the left (east), and intersects CR 7, also known as Church Avenue. Take CR 7 right (south).

21.2   Ride into Union Hill, a hamlet with a graceful Catholic church, St. John's.

The parish welcomes visitors. Note also the baseball park for the Union Hill Bulldogs, a Minnesota "field of dreams."

21.3   Turn left (east) onto MN 19.

23.9   Note the restored classic brick edifice on your left. See the nearby "energy house" built into the hillside.

25.7   Arrive in New Prague, ride to Main Street and your car.

This was a western-style slice of Twin City life.

Bicycle Repair Service

The nearest one is 14 miles southeast of your starting point in New Prague:

Dave's Bike Clinic, 13753 Echo Avenue, Lonsdale, 507-334-9743

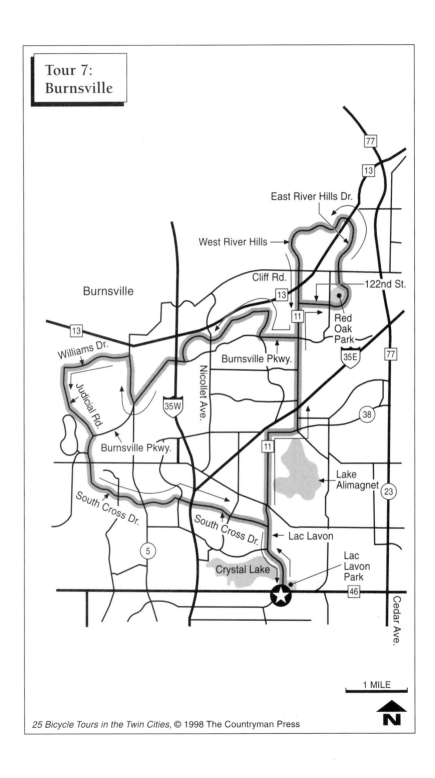

Tour 7:
Burnsville

77
13

East River Hills Dr.

West River Hills

Cliff Rd.

Burnsville

13

122nd St.

13

11

Red
Oak
Park

35E

77

Williams Dr.

Burnsville Pkwy.

Nicollet Ave.

35W

38

Judicial Rd.

Burnsville Pkwy.

Lake
Alimagnet

23

South Cross Dr.

South Cross Dr.

Lac Lavon

5

Crystal Lake

Lac
Lavon
Park

11

46

Cedar Ave.

1 MILE

N

25 Bicycle Tours in the Twin Cities, © 1998 The Countryman Press

7

Burnsville

Distance: 24.5 miles
Terrain: Flat to easy rolling hills; some active motor traffic and some marked bicycle trails, usually on sidewalks
Location: Dakota County
Special features: Classic upscale suburbia, small parks, skyline of Minneapolis, Burnsville Center Mall

This tour takes you through much of the everyday life of the area, as well as past its scenic wonders. In Burnsville, daily life is something very close to the American dream, at least on the surface: there are heavily wooded lots; an abundance of city parks, lakes, churches, and specialty shops; and excellent schools. It has the Twin City qualities of accessibility, variety, and unity. Local pride flourishes around the winning records of high school athletics. Its government promotes progressive programs for community recreation. A comprehensive bicycle trail plan covers the entire city; your ride stretches to its four corners.

Super suburbs such as this have services and an ambience all their own. What they lack in nostalgia, old buildings, and coziness, they replace with rambling modern homes, pocket-sized parks, lots of trees, and large lawns.

To park, take Cedar Avenue (which is also CR 23 if coming from the south and MN 77 if coming from the north), to CR 46. Turn west (left, if coming from the south, right if coming from the north), and drive 1.3 miles to CR 11. Turn right (north) onto CR 11. Find Lac Lavon Park and leave your car there. The park is large and accessible.

Suburban bliss in Burnsville

0.0   Leave Lac Lavon Park and turn right onto Lac Lavon Drive.

0.7   Pass a sign pointing to Crystal Lake.

Just to your left you can see the lake, one of the major ones in the area.

1.1   Turn right onto CR 11, which begins out of Lac Lavon Drive, and head north on it.

1.9   Note the Center for the Arts.

You'll soon enjoy a great view of Lake Alimagnet with its protected, native vegetation. Here CR 11 is marked as a bicycle trail.

4.5   Cross a major road, Burnsville Parkway, but continue to head north on CR 11, which will take you to the northeast corner of Burnsville.

4.8   Turn right (east) onto 122nd Street, which is the access road for East River Hills Drive.

This is the heart of Burnsville, with wide streets, old trees, and

manicured lawns. The city is protecting the trees. This road becomes East River Hills Drive, as the signs indicate.

6.6   Pass Red Oak Park.

You could stop here for rest rooms, running water, and picnic
tables.

**7.2   Come to a major artery, Cliff Road; cross it and continue on
East River Hills Drive.**

At the northernmost point of this loop you cross MN 13. This is a
busy intersection with a stop light; dismount and walk across it,
then head west, still on the marked East River Hills Drive.

**8.4   Note this road turns into West River Hills Drive. Continue on it
as it turns south and heads toward CR 11.**

**9.8   Turn right (west) onto Burnsville Parkway. You'll come to the
marked bicycle trail. Turn right onto the trail where it leaves
the parkway and ride on it.**

Note how the city uses ponds, trees, and hills to help the housing
blend into the landscape.

**13.1   Cross a major intersection, Nicollet Avenue. Continue on the
bike path, which parallels Burnsville Parkway.**

**14.0   When you intersect I-35W, ride over it into the older part of
Burnsville.**

**15.0   Turn right (north) onto CR 5 and ride on it to the northwest
corner of Burnsville.**

Notice the fine view of the Minneapolis skyline.

16.2   Turn left (west) onto Williams Drive.

Enjoy the beautiful vistas along the way.

17.3   Turn left (south) onto Judicial Road.

Notice a cemetery here, a sight not often seen in new suburbs.

19.3   Go slightly right, south, onto South Cross Drive.

This is the final leg of the four-corner loop.

20.8   See Burnsville Center Mall, one of the first malls in Minnesota.

Stay on South Cross Drive, clearly marked as both a sidewalk and
a bicycle trail. Pass under I-35W.

23.8 Turn right (south) onto Lac Lavon Drive, and return to Lac Lavon Park.

24.5 You've returned to your car.

Bicycle Repair Service

Erik's Bike Shop, 14613 CR 11, Burnsville, 612-891-6411

8

Apple Valley–Rosemount

Distance: 17.6 miles
Terrain: Flat to easy rolling hills; some active motor traffic
Location: Dakota County
Special features: Parks, lakes, state-of-the-art public school buildings

The two communities along this ride are south suburbs, freestanding from Minneapolis or St. Paul, with their own personalities. Although they border each other, each has its distinctive charms. Excellent, clearly marked bike paths make getting to know these towns a pleasure.

Apple Valley is a highly progressive, rapidly expanding suburb. It has parks, walkways, and attractive subdivisions. It wants to grow. Rosemount, however, stands pat, content with its small-town traits, excellent schools, and quiet neighborhoods.

To park, find the intersection of CR 23 (Cedar Avenue) and CR 42 in Apple Valley. Then find the Target Store on the east strip mall (on the right-hand side of CR 42) and park in the lot there.

0.0 Go right (east) on CR 42, along a classic shopping strip.

Be encouraged that with all the suburban dependence on automobiles, the civic planners are still giving us bicycle trails!

0.1 Ride on the north side of CR 42.

Pedestrians use this lane also.

0.2 Pass a gravel pit and some light industry.

3.0 Cross Pilot Knob Road (CR 31) and presto! You are out in farmland with fields of corn and soybeans.

4.4 Arrive in Rosemount. Turn left (north) onto MN 3 and ride on the right side.

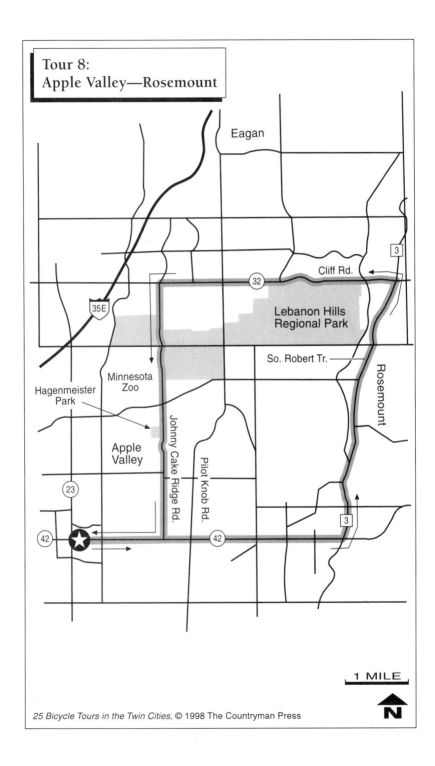

Tour 8:
Apple Valley—Rosemount

Eagan

35E

3

Cliff Rd.

32

Lebanon Hills
Regional Park

So. Robert Tr.

Rosemount

Minnesota
Zoo

Hagenmeister
Park

Apple
Valley

Johnny Cake Ridge Rd.

Pilot Knob Rd.

23

42

42

3

1 MILE

N

25 Bicycle Tours in the Twin Cities, © 1998 The Countryman Press

ERLING JORSTAD

Granddaughters Jessica and Krista on their way to the zoo.

4.5 *Enter the heart of Rosemount, with its Irish-motif street banners.*

5.5 *Note the shops and stores.*

Most have been here for decades and are doing well, even with heavyweights such as the Mall of America nearby. Note St. Joseph's Catholic Church, old and dignified.

5.8 *See the centerpiece, the Rosemount public school buildings.*

This school district has expanded rapidly to meet the huge increase in population. It offers sports, drama, music, and related activities, all of which help strengthen civic pride. You may want to ride around the school, something of a model for other Twin City suburbs as they expand.

6.1 *Observe the red, white, and blue barber-pole stripes on the silo.*

This is gracious, rural-home country with few condominiums.

Most of the houses are located on a large number of tiny lakes or ponds. Although not very good for boating or fishing, the ponds still give the suburb a country aura.

7.7 *You enter Eagan, another hugely growing suburb.*

8.7 *Turn left (west) onto Cliff Road, also known as CR 32.*

Here find several bicycle trails and the entrance to Lebanon Hills Regional Park, which has trails, picnic tables, and rest rooms.

12.4 *At Thomas Lake Center Mall, turn left (south) onto Johnny Cake Ridge Road and head for the Minnesota Zoo.*

This is an ideal road for riding—smooth, wide, and with excellent shoulders. It rises and falls in a nice rhythm.

13.9 *Ride past the city limits of Apple Valley.*

14.7 *Find the sign pointing to the Minnesota Zoo.*

A state treasure, the zoo is certainly worth a stop. Admission is $8 for adults; $5 for seniors; $4 for children.

15.1 *Pass Hagenmeister Park, small but inviting, on your right.*

16.0 *Pass the local school in Apple Valley, which, as in Rosemount, is the community center.*

Note the size and extensive equipment of the athletic facilities.

17.0 *Turn right (west) onto CR 42.*

17.6 *You're back at the Target parking lot and your car.*

Bicycle Repair Service

Valley Bike Shop, 7707 149th Street NW, Apple Valley, 612-432-1666

9

St. Paul

Distance: *34.6 miles*
Terrain: *Flat to gently rolling with two overpass rides; all on the Gateway State Trail except for one short on-road jaunt.*
Location: *Washington and Ramsey Counties*
Special features: *Outing Lodge, rural and urban scenic vistas*

The countryside around St. Paul has its own distinct features. It embraces long stretches of wooded, often marshy land; some excellent farmland; and widely separated homes. You'll find trails for horseback riding and places for bird-watching. The wildflowers bloom in great profusion around the roadside ditches.

Yet as this trail shows, the rural, suburban, and urban parts of the saintly city are in close proximity. Be ready for rapid transitions as you ride; the Gateway State Trail, maintained by the State Department of Transportation, moves quickly from isolated woodlands into suburbia, and reaches its turnaround point less than 3 miles from downtown St. Paul. You'll pedal close to some impressive lakes, and pass by a lesser known but distinguished country inn, the Outing Lodge.

Thus this bike trail is, as the local riders call it, the gateway to greater St. Paul. Tables, rest rooms, and water are available; for snacking, you'll ride by a number of suburban eateries.

To park, take CR 5 north, then west, from Stillwater. Turn north onto CR 55 and drive for 5 miles. Park at the clearly marked Pine Point Park. The new, handsome park building has all necessary facilities.

0.0 *Ride west on the Gateway Trail, watching for the horse trail.*
    Equestrians are instructed not to bring their steeds on the Gateway.

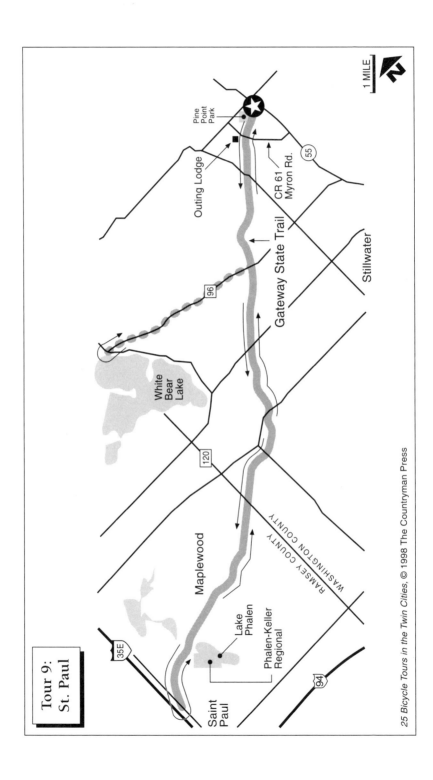

Tour 9:
St. Paul

Pine Point Park

Outing Lodge

CR 61
Myron Rd.

55

Gateway State Trail

Stillwater

96

White
Bear
Lake

120

Maplewood

RAMSEY COUNTY
WASHINGTON COUNTY

Lake
Phalen

Phalen-Keller
Regional

35E

Saint Paul

94

1 MILE

25 Bicycle Tours in the Twin Cities, © 1998 The Countryman Press

0.3   *Notice the bluebird houses on fence posts.*

There are many birch trees and the terrain is marshy.

1.2   *Turn right (west) onto CR 61 (also known as Myron Road) and go 0.1 mile. Follow the signs to the Outing Lodge at Pine Point.*

Do look around in this large mansion, now a country inn and banquet center. The lush flower gardens are filled with my favorites, hollyhocks. The lodge staff are very low key; employees will answer your questions, but will leave you to roam at your leisure. The huge fireplace is worth a photograph. The inn is most popular for weddings, receptions, and conferences.

1.4   *Return to the trail and turn right.*

3.2   *Note the dense, marshy woods, quite unusual for this area.*

5.5   *Intersect MN 96. Continue on the trail.*

This highway is the major artery between Stillwater and White Bear Lake, a tour you may want to take later. On your right, in about a mile, is the new and up-to-date Mahtomedi public school complex. Note how the environs start to change. Perhaps a few white horses, monuments to the past, can still be seen in the pastures on your left.

8.9   *Pass through the tunnel for MN 36, an unusual highway structure.*

10.1   *Ride under I-694.*

12.3   *Cross MN 120, also known as Century Avenue, which is the dividing line between Washington and Ramsey Counties.*

13.4   *Be ready to stop here at the McKnight Road overpass bridge. Your way is bumpy, but a nice contrast to the smooth roads so far.*

McKnight is the family name for 3M, a large manufacturer in east St. Paul, best known for Scotch brand tape.

15.4   *Ride into Maplewood, a well-maintained suburb.*

You'll pass several homes, parks, and playgrounds.

16.4   *Approach Lake Phalen and the Phalen-Keller Regional Park.*

A Mississippi river boat enters St. Paul

©MINNESOTA OFFICE OF TOURISM

This would be a pleasant side jaunt of about an hour; the route is clearly marked.

17.1 Find the second overpass, known as the Wheelock Parkway Bridge.

This, too, is bumpy.

17.3 Arrive at the turnaround point on the Gateway Trail.

The view of the downtown skyline is excellent. You will find a rest room here, and an information kiosk. After a rest, turn around and head back to Pine Point Park through this nicely varied slice of St. Paul.

34.6 You're back at your car.

Bicycle Repair Service

St. Croix Bicycle & Skate, 1876 Tower Drive, Stillwater, 612-439-2337

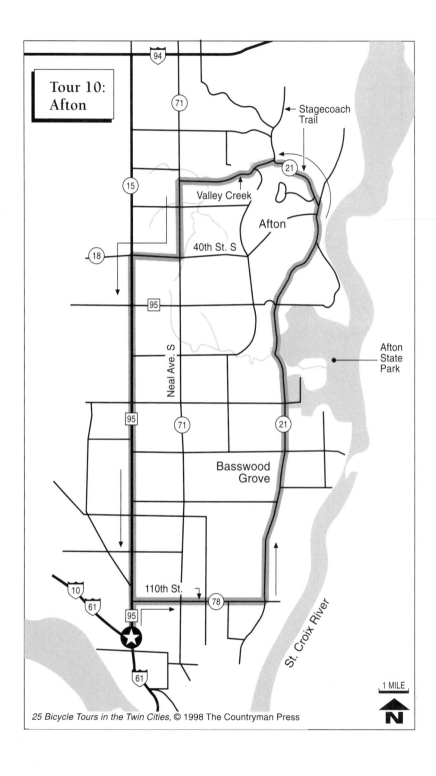

Tour 10:
Afton

94

71

Stagecoach
Trail

21

15

Valley Creek

Afton

40th St. S

18

95

Neal Ave. S

Afton
State
Park

95

71

21

Basswood
Grove

110th St.

10

61

95

78

61

St. Croix River

1 MILE

N

25 Bicycle Tours in the Twin Cities, © 1998 The Countryman Press

10

Afton

Distance: *27.8 miles*
Terrain: *Flat to hilly; two long descents; light auto traffic*
Location: *Washington County*
Special features: *Afton State Park, St. Croix River, village of Afton*

Robert Burns, the Scots poet, would be pleased to know that this town was named after the lyric "Flow gently sweet Afton" from his famous poem "Afton Water." This is a lovely, nestled-in village east of St. Paul, yet very much a part of the Twin Cities. The town itself is inhabited by only a few hundred people, while the surrounding countryside pops and crackles during the growing season with corn, grain, and soybeans. The whole ambience is reminiscent of a bygone era when there was one, but only one, of each kind of store: deli, ice cream, antiques, and toys. Yet at the same time, Afton's agriculture shows its successful adaptation to high technology.

The region also makes great use of its matchless treasure, the St. Croix River. The locals have kept its shores free from development. You'll also find here a state park with a wonderful view of the river valley. The zoning laws encourage urbanites to build imaginative getaway homes that harmonize with the hilly forests and open valleys. Yet the bustling world of St. Paul is only a few miles away, with the rich cultural resources of Minneapolis also nearby. Afton has chosen to stay as it is, and extends a warm welcome to bicycle riders.

To park, heading east on I-94 turn right (south) onto CR 15 and go 3.8 miles. At MN 95, go south for 5.9 miles to the intersection with US 61. Find Valley Suburban Auto Works at that intersection, and park in the large nearby lot. Or head north on US 61 out of Hastings (see Tour 11) to MN 95. Park at the Valley Suburban Auto Works lot.

ERLING JORSTAD

Selma's of Afton

0.0 Ride north on CR 95.

0.7 Turn right (east) onto CR 78, also known as 110th Street.

This gets you out into the countryside right away, where special attention is paid to dairy production.

1.6 Notice the dairy farm here.

1.9 Note the gorgeous orchard on the right.

The land here, with its sandy soil, warm days, cool nights, and abundance of water, is ideal for apples.

2.1 Pass quirky mailbox art.

3.4 CR 78 ends. Turn left (north) onto MN 21.

4.1 Note a remarkably well-kept traditional home on your left.

The small buildings by the driveways along here are shelters for children waiting in the cold for school buses. Sometimes the buildings are turned into summer playhouses.

6.4 You are on the brow of the first major descent; be ready.

7.1   At the sign for Afton State Park, turn right and ride to the main entrance.

This facility has lots of hiking trails for viewing the natural habitat, the St. Croix Valley, and for picnicking. As with all state parks, an entrance fee is charged.

8.3   You are at the main entrance.

There's a public telephone here. Take time to search out the views of this beautiful valley.

8.4   Make a U-turn; see the Afton Alps Ski Center.

In the summer, Afton Alps opens its 7 miles of grassy trails to serious mountain bikers. An admission fee is charged.

8.5   Backtrack to MN 21 and turn right.

8.8   See the golf course and St. Mary's Episcopal Church.

9.6   The curving roads, unique to this region, make for rewarding riding.

12.7   Enter Afton.

The town is filled with wonderful old houses, many recently restored. Take a break to look around at the shops and visit Selma's ice cream parlor, which is rich in history. You won't find tourist traps here. The Afton House, an inn and restaurant, has been in business since 1867.

13.2   Head north on MN 21, then turn left (west) onto Stagecoach Trail.

14.4   Turn left (west) onto Valley Creek Trail.

Note the elegant houses and fast-running creeks here.

15.4   Turn left (south) onto Neal Avenue (CR 71).

16.4   Turn right (west) onto CR 18 (also known as 40th Street South, or Bailey Road).

17.0   Find a great array of imaginative homes at the corner.

17.2   Turn left (south) onto MN 95.

This is a superb ride through rich farmland. Note the several nurseries with varied plants for sale.

25.0 Find the junction with CR 78 and the apple orchard advertising "pick your own"; continue riding south on MN 95.

27.8 You're back at Valley Suburban Auto Works and your car.
Return to US 61 if headed south to Hastings, or go north on US 61 to get to I-94.

Bicycle Repair Service

Valley Bike Shop, US 61 and MN 95, Hastings; 612-438-3644

PART THREE:
OLD MAN RIVER

Old Man River

Among the many delightful, often breathtaking (and not from uphill riding) features of southeast Minnesota are the tours around the cities on the Mississippi River. From its origin in Lake Itasca far to the north, the river hits its stride in the Twin Cities and comes into its own as a major force in shaping the lives of residents near its waters.

The contrasts for its people in their lifestyles, their natural settings, their weather, and their economic strivings are great. You ride alongside barges and boxcars headed for St. Louis or New Orleans. Yet 2 miles to the west, you ride through rich farmlands and quiet villages. Here's another contrast: The high hills near the river are very close to flat pastureland. Or note, when you are riding, the heavy river traffic of watercraft, and the wildlife refuges, grain elevators, and riverside eateries standing very close to township roads with narrow bridges and isolated homes. Notice as well that buildings and transportation here are constructed so as to survive both howling winter storms and hot, humid summer days.

These four cities—Hastings, Red Wing, Lake City, and Wabasha—owe their existence to the many local businesses that take the inland's rich farm produce, process it in elevators and mills, and send it on its way to world markets. The many services—agricultural, industrial, business, civic, and educational—that attend these transactions are what gives each city its distinct character.

Yet our quartet of towns shares several traits, the most visible and impressive for bicyclists being their distinctive blend of old and new. All feature historic buildings that are listed on the National Register; at the same time local businesses rely on high-tech river navigation and other electronic wizardry to remain competitive in the late twentieth century.

Finally, all four towns offer friendly, well-marked streets, shops, and services for adventurous riders along Old Man River.

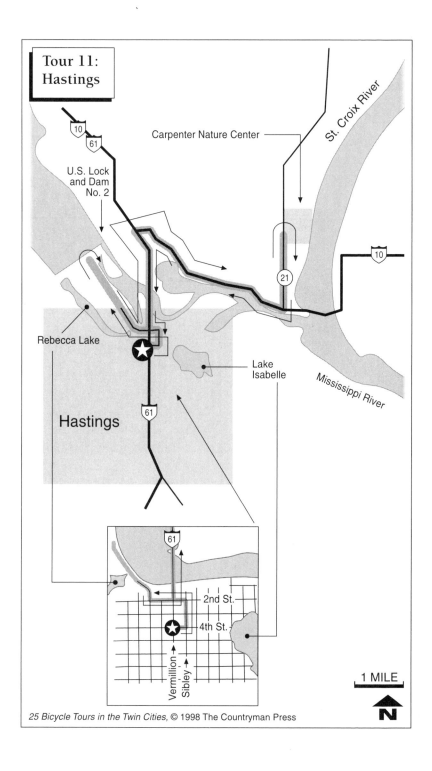

Tour 11:
Hastings

St. Croix River

Carpenter Nature Center

U.S. Lock
and Dam
No. 2

61

Rebecca Lake

Lake
Isabelle

Mississippi River

Hastings

61

2nd St.

4th St.

Vermillion

Sibley

1 MILE

N

25 Bicycle Tours in the Twin Cities, © 1998 The Countryman Press

11

Hastings

Distance: 15.1 miles
Terrain: Flat to very hilly; some city auto traffic
Location: Dakota County
Special features: Historic buildings; U.S. Lock and Dam No. 2;
   Carpenter Nature Center

The four tours in this section go from north to south along the river. You start with the beautiful and historic Hastings. Combining a remarkable dedication to preserving its past and also offering an attractive city for the present, Hastings is a full day's discovery for the rider. Though short in distance, this tour is rich in restored homes and businesses; it has a Mississippi River lock and dam complex, a sparkling marina, and a rewarding nature center. All that in 15.1 miles! In addition, you may want to consider side trips to Spring Lake Park Preserve (612-438-4460 or 612-438-4671) and, farther south, the Alexis Bailly Vineyard (612-437-1413).

To park, enter Hastings on US 61, and find the intersection of Vermillion Street (US 61) and Fourth Street in the center of Hastings. There you will find the Hastings City Hall, formerly the Dakota County Courthouse, a splendid edifice in the Italianate style. Park at the lot there.

0.0   *From the intersection of Fourth and Vermillion, go left (east) onto Fourth Street.*

Note the restored St. Elizabeth Anne Seaton Catholic Church and the nearby Guardian Angels Chapel.

0.1   *Turn left (north) onto Sibley Street.*

0.3   *This is the heart of the restored district.*

The bicycle trail along the river in Hastings

Take your time here; most buildings are on the National Register of Historic Sites, and worth a closer look. At Second Street you are right by the river and at the center of the old town.

0.7   *When ready, head west on Second Street and go under the bridge. Find the bicycle trail by the river.*

Barges and other watercraft are daily attractions here. I am always amazed at the navigational skills of the bargemasters.

0.9   *Still on the bicycle trail, continue northwest.*

1.6   *You're at Lock and Dam No. 2.*

It's worth the wait to see river craft of any size go through here. The navigational pool formed by U.S. Lock and Dam No. 2 is 33 miles in length and extends back into St. Paul, making it one of the river's largest ports. You'll find water, picnic tables, and rest rooms nearby.

1.6   *Make a U-turn and head back to Hastings.*

2.2   *Turn left onto Second Street, noting the sign pointing to US 61 North. You will be taking that highway.*

3.6 *Turn left onto US 61 North. Cross the bridge, a major adventure.*

Caution: This is a very busy road, so walking it is recommended, but savor the panorama either way.

4.2 *Back on terra firma, head up US 61 and up a good-sized hill.*

Although the ascent is steep, there are excellent shoulders for riding.

5.0 *See the sign pointing to Prescott, Wisconsin. Pass it, then turn right (east) onto US 10.*

Be ready for great views.

6.1 *Go down a rather steep hill.*

8.1 *Turn left (north) onto CR 21 and start up a good-sized hill.*

You are near the confluence of the Mississippi and St. Croix Rivers.

9.0 *You arrive at Carpenter Nature Center.*

This is a privately funded, 600-acre preserve with breathtaking views of the St. Croix River. The center (612-437-4359) has full-time naturalists, displays, an interpretive center, and 15 miles of well-marked hiking trails. It is most definitely a must-see, your reward for having pedaled so hard to get here.

9.0 *Return now the same way to Hastings: Go south on CR 21 to US 10 to US 61 South, and return to the City Hall at Vermillion and Fourth Street.*

It's a double dose of a great river city. For a side trip, you may later want to ride to Prescott, Wisconsin, on CR 10, a very pleasant destination.

15.0 *You are back at your car.*

Alternate routes: The Spring Lake Park Preserve is located on CR 42, five miles west of Lock and Dam No. 2. (This bike ride doesn't go along CR 42.) The Alexis Bailly Vineyard is 1 mile south of Hastings on US 61. Turn right at 170th Street and follow the road for 2 miles.

Bicycle Repair Service

Valley Bike Shop, MN 95 and US 61, Hastings; 612-438-3644

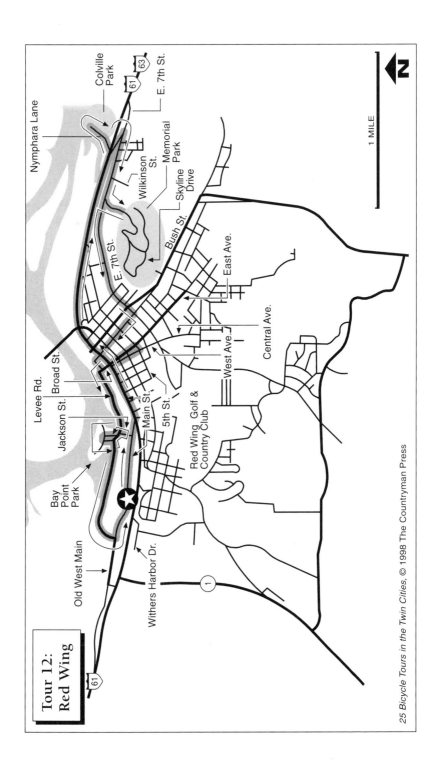

Tour 12:
Red Wing

61

Nymphara Lane

Colville Park

61

63

E. 7th St.

Wilkinson St.

Memorial Park

Skyline Drive

Bush St.

E. 7th St.

East Ave.

Central Ave.

West Ave.

Levee Rd.

Broad St.

Jackson St.

Main St.

5th St.

Red Wing Golf & Country Club

Bay Point Park

Old West Main

Withers Harbor Dr.

1

N

1 MILE

25 Bicycle Tours in the Twin Cities, © 1998 The Countryman Press

12

Red Wing

Distance: *9.9 miles*
Terrain: *Flat to very hilly; moderate street traffic*
Location: *Goodhue County*
Special features: *River marina, grain elevators, city parks, Look Out Scenic Drive, restored Victorian-era buildings; Barn Bluff Look Out; Red Wing Shoes*

This gem offers the bicyclist a chance to ride through a city from top to bottom: from exquisite vistas to river marinas; from distinguished civic malls to the backyards of those whose town is named for the red-winged blackbird. In miles, this trail is short; in terms of opportunities for finding treasures and spin-off rides, it is quite long.

Red Wing first flourished as a shipping destination from the rich heartlands of Goodhue County (see Tours 20, 23, and 24). At the mouth of the Cannon River and as a major railroad departure point to Chicago, it grew into a lively community, attracting a variety of immigrants and native-born transplants. Today its charm is in its parks, its pottery warehouse district, its dignified downtown restoration, and its skyline drives. Its most famous buildings are the beautifully appointed St. James Hotel and the resplendent T.B. Sheldon Theatre, both built at the turn of the century. Along Fourth and Pine stand several distinguished mansions that are well worth a visit.

To park, from US 61, just north of downtown, turn east onto West Main Street. Park at the Pottery Place lot. One-half mile west of here you can connect with the Cannon Valley Trail (see Tour 2).

0.0   Leave the parking lot and head east on Old West Main Street.

0.2   See signs pointing to Bay Point Park.

0.6   Turn left onto Jackson Street. Turn left again onto Levee Road and ride on it for about 20 yards.

On your right, find the entrance to Bay Point Park. This park has excellent paths for bicycling. Cruise the park at will; find picnic tables and rest rooms, and views of the grain elevators near the railroads and the river.

1.0   Ride out of the park and retrace your path. Turn left (east) onto Old West Main Street.

1.1   At the stoplight turn left (east) onto Main Street (US 61).

1.5   At the stoplight, turn right (south) onto West Avenue.

This is Red Wing at its best, the town center much like those in New England. Note the distinguished blend of civic and church buildings.

1.8   Turn left (northeast) onto Fifth Street and ride one block.

1.9   Turn left (northwest) onto East Avenue.

This is the other side of the city square.

2.1   See on your right one of the great buildings, the restored T.B. Sheldon Theatre, at Third Street and East Avenue.

2.2   Turn right (east) back onto Main Street (US 61) and ride through the heart of downtown.

You are now on a combination of Main Street, US 61, and US 63. Stay on it.

3.7   Headed toward Colville Park, you'll see MN 292 on your right. Turn right at the sign onto MN 292.

3.8   See the sign for Colville Park. (See also the Days Inn as a reference check.) Make a U-turn. You are on East Seventh Street.

3.9   Turn right (east) onto Nymphara Lane and ride through the underpass under Main Street and US 61/US 63.

4.0   You are in Colville Park.

Colville has all facilities; explore at your leisure. You are right alongside the Mississippi River.

River bluffs overlook the town of Red Wing.

4.1 *Make a U-turn. Return to Nymphara Lane and ride through the underpass back to East Seventh Street.*

4.2 *Turn right (west) onto East Seventh Street. Pass Wilkinson Street on your left; keep riding on East Seventh Street.*

4.3 *Turn left at the sign for Memorial Park and ride through the entrance gates and up a steep hill on Skyline Drive. The top of the hill is 0.7 miles away. I advise you walk at least part of it (it's fun coming down!).*

5.0 *You are very near the top, your destination.*

See the graystone Tower. This will be your landmark to show you where to find your way down. Enjoy the sumptuous scenery of what is known as the Hiawatha Valley. You see Wisconsin, you see all of Red Wing as you ride around, perhaps you will even see tomorrow. The Look Out Scenic Drive area has picnic tables, restrooms, and barbecues; also find markers pointing out some distant town sites.

5.4 *Staying on the main road, ride around this loop at your leisure.*

Note that near the Tower descent exit, you'll find on your right another descending road. This could be an additional loop for you. It goes for 0.4 miles (not included in the mileage for this ride), half of which is downhill! It comes back to the Tower exit.

5.8 *Arrive back at the Tower exit. Continue riding on the right side of the road.*

Enjoy the trip downhill, you've earned it.

6.5 *Ride through the Memorial Park entrance/exit gate, and turn left (west) onto East Seventh Street.*

You're back on flat ground again.

6.8 *Continue on East Seventh Street.*

You are on a major street, featuring well-kept homes, wonderful gardens, and individualized house decorations.

7.9 *Turn right (northwest) onto Bush Street, another major artery.*

Ride on Bush to the heart of the downtown.

8.4 *Cross Main Street/US 61.*

You have been here before. You see at 404 Main Street the other great building, the St. James Hotel. Excellent specialty shops are nearby.

8.5 *Continue on Bush Street, crossing Main/US 61.*

You go down a slight hill here.

8.6 *You arrive at the railroad tracks and the train depot. Turn left (west) onto Levee Street and ride for one block, going by the depot.*

Inside is the city's chamber of commerce. Here you'll find maps, information, and facilities.

8.7 *Turn right onto Broad Street and find the sign pointing to Levee Park.*

At Levee Park you'll find senior citizens passing the time of day, children playing on park facilities, and everyone watching the extensive rivercraft traffic.

8.8 *At Levee Park, find the sign for Levee Road. Turn left (west) and ride on that road.*

Here you'll see several grain elevators. My ancestors in the 1870s took their grain via oxcart to this location.

9.6   *Levee Road curves left here.*

9.8   *Go up a slight hill and intersect Withers Harbor Drive at a stop sign. See the Pottery Place parking lot. You are now at its west end and your car is at its east end.*

9.9   *Ride through the parking lot to your car.*

Bicycle Repair Service

Outdoor Store, 323 Main Street, Red Wing; 612-388-5358

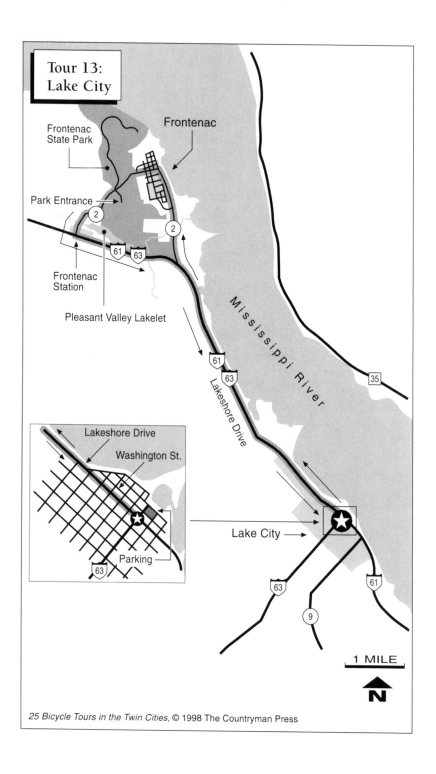

Tour 13:
Lake City

Frontenac State Park

Frontenac

Park Entrance

Frontenac Station

Pleasant Valley Lakelet

Mississippi River

Lakeshore Drive

Lakeshore Drive

Washington St.

Parking

Lake City

1 MILE

N

25 Bicycle Tours in the Twin Cities, © 1998 The Countryman Press

13

Lake City

Distance: 17.1 miles
Terrain: Flat to gentle hills; light traffic
Location: Goodhue and Wabasha Counties
Special features: Lake Pepin, Old Frontenac, Frontenac State Park

This trip may be done in a half day. For a full day, combine it with the ride around Wabasha (Tour 14). Lake City, with its 5000 residents, has successfully utilized the river's resources to enhance its quality of life. Its focus is Lake Pepin, which is actually part of the Mississippi River, but at a point where it becomes 3 miles wide, stretching southward for 21 miles—a lake within a river.

The lake's claim to fame is that in 1922, an 18-year-old named Ralph W. Samuelson invented waterskiing here. He strapped two boards to his feet, entered the lake, and let a motorized boat take him for a ride at high speed.

Today Lake City has an annual summer festival called Water Ski Days and has built what is the largest marina for private recreation on the entire Mississippi River, locating it just two blocks from downtown. It serves as the "port" for many landlocked cities, including Rochester.

The surrounding countryside, especially to the north, embraces some spectacular scenery for riding and bird-watching. Minnesota State Park attracts large numbers of visitors with its natural habitat, game refuges, and hiking trails.

Within the city, you find attractive homes and some well-restored churches at the city commons. The spic-and-span, 3-mile-long Lakeshore Drive welcomes walkers, joggers, and sightseers within city limits to view the glories of the lake.

©MINNESOTA OFFICE OF TOURISM

The Lake City marina

To park, find the junction of US 61 and US 63 in downtown Lake City. Park at the marina just east of this junction, located at Lyon and Washington Streets. View the lake from here before riding.

0.0 *Starting at Lyon Street, return to the US 61–US 63 junction and turn right (north) onto US 61/US 63, also known as Lakeshore Drive.*

1.2 *Out in the open country, notice some very high bluffs on the left. These are often homes for eagles.*

2.7 *Find a gorgeous view of the lake, at its widest here, with boats, birds, and fishing folks galore.*

4.0 *Find a complete rest area with all facilities, built in 1996.*

4.8 *See some tall oak trees here.*

4.9 *Take a right (north) onto CR 2 and ride along it into the woods.*

5.7 Find the sign OLD FRONTENAC HISTORIC DISTRICT, which signals a trail highlight.

Two Jesuit missionaries founded the Mission St. Michael the Archangel in this region in the 1700s. By 1840, permanent settlement by Europeans was established with the founding of the town of Frontenac. The spectacular view of Lake Pepin attracted many visitors and in the 1870s a community started to grow. It soon became a popular summer resort area with expensive homes. From there it evolved into a dignified, serene, year-round place of residence for about 50 families. They have maintained its low-key charm. This tour takes you through the town.

5.8 Turn left at the sign pointing to Villa Maria Academy.

Tour the academy on foot. This Catholic convent was founded in the 1870s. The original building burned down, but a new and handsome edifice is now used mostly for retreats, conferences, and spiritual renewal. Note its French architecture.

6.1 Back on CR 2, ride to the town center, where you'll find interesting lawn art.

6.8 Take your time to ride around at your leisure; you can't get lost.

7.4 See the Episcopal church, a landmark.

7.6 Turn right onto CR 28, the entrance road to Frontenac State Park. Ride there, only a few yards.

This is a state park, with an entry fee (612-345-3401). It has 15 miles of well-kept hiking trails for up-close viewing of the varied vegetation. It is famous for its bird habitat; during the months without snow on the ground some 200 species of birds have been observed here.

7.7 Back outside the park, from CR 28 turn right (south) onto CR 2.

9.8 Turn left (south) onto US 61/US 63.

This last leg brings you past a flea market, a fudge factory(!), and fast-food outlets.

17.1 You are back at your car at Lyon and Washington Streets.
  You might want to continue riding to the west, seeing fine old steepled churches and the town center.

Bicycle Repair Service

The nearest repair stop is 17 miles north of Lake City:

Outdoor Store, 323 Main Street, Red Wing; 612-388-5358

14

Wabasha

Distance: 17.1 miles
Terrain: Flat to gently rolling hills; light to moderate traffic
Location: Wabasha County
Special features: River bridge, Anderson House, Saint Felix Catholic Church, National Wildlife Refuge Center, river bluffs

Life along the river takes figurative as well as literal turns. Once a booming river town, Wabasha's population has stabilized at 4000. The community is proud of its past and happy to stay small. It welcomes the old-time classic steamboats *Delta Queen* and *Mississippi Queen* on their periodic stops. It proudly points to its new bridge spanning the river, the only one between Red Wing and Winona. It's proud that its train depot was photographed for the introduction of the movie *Grumpy Old Men* (while acknowledging that most of the filming was done elsewhere in the state).

Wabasha has one of the region's first hotels, the circa-1850 Anderson House, as well as several other restored buildings on the National Register. The town's other attractions include outdoor festivals during summer months, Saint Felix Catholic Church, and a National Wildlife Refuge Center, designed to protect birds migrating on their way from Canada to points south. In Wabasha the bicyclist has much to discover of old and new, as well as the pleasures of the outdoors. As suggested in Tour 13, this tour can be done in a half day, then paired with Lake City for a full day of riding.

To park, take US 61 north or south to Wabasha, then turn onto CR 30, which is also Hiawatha Drive. Park at Norm's Super Valu lot, where

Tour 14:
Wabasha

Mississippi River

61

30

Robinson
Lake

60

24

24

24

Peterson
Lake

Spring
Street

Main St.

60

Pembroke Ave.

30

61

60

Hiawatha Dr.

30

Upper
Mississippi
River
National
Wildlife &
Fish Refuge

61

1 MILE

N

25 Bicycle Tours in the Twin Cities, © 1998 The Countryman Press

CR 30 and CR 60 intersect. You take two rides here, the first through town, the other through the countryside.

0.0   *Start by riding north on CR 60, also called Pembroke Avenue*

Note the Tourist Information Center just as you start out. Riding ahead you come to Saint Felix Church, a magnificent stone structure in excellent condition. It's worth a look.

0.3   *Across the street, see Grace Memorial Episcopal Church.*

Tours are available by appointment (612-565-2170).

0.4   *Arrive at the intersection with Main Street, the heart of Wabasha.*

Allow time to savor the shops, some more than 100 years old. This is a living museum of early Minnesota history. Too numerous to list separately, these buildings are on the National Register. Of special interest is Dick's Uptown Art Gallery, at 164 Pembroke Avenue.

0.6   *Turn left onto Main Street and view the Mississippi River bridge entrance.*

You might want to pedal up it. You'll pass the Anderson House, 333 North Main Street, owned by the same family for four generations. It has 45 rooms and many thoughtfully assembled antiques. It is open to the public for tours (1-800-535-5467).

0.7   *Turn left (south) left onto Bridge Avenue.*

See Saint Felix from another angle. Note that Bridge Avenue becomes Spring Street.

1.4   *Turn left (east) onto CR 30 (Hiawatha Drive) and ride back past Norm's Super Valu and your car.*

See another part of Wabasha's tidy residential area.

2.3   *Pass the cemetery for Saint Felix's, on your left, and head out into the countryside on an excellent road for biking.*

3.7   *Notice the consolidated public schools.*

As with many towns, this is the community center. This integrated school system thrives with efficient technology and transportation.

4.5   *Turn left (east) onto CR 24. This provides a loop through suburban Wabasha, taking you close to the river and past quiet backyards.*

The Anderson House Inn in Wabasha

©MINNESOTA OFFICE OF TOURISM

5.9   Follow CR 24 as it bends right (south).

7.8   You see the Mississippi from here; the fishing is good.

7.9   Arrive at the Upper Mississippi River National Wildlife and Fish Refuge Center.

The information kiosk here is very helpful.

8.4   Continue west on CR 24, noting the food store.

9.3   Arrive in open country, wonderfully flat.

11.2   Turn right (north) onto US 61 (this is the route you took if you came in from the south).

From here back to Wabasha, take special notice of the stunning high bluffs on your left (much like those on Tour 1) with thick woods and a wide variety of wildflowers and other foliage. The views are spectacular.

15.0   Turn right onto CR 60 and ride back to Norm's Super Valu.

17.1   You're back at your car.

Bicycle Repair Service

The nearest service is 26 miles north, in Red Wing:

Outdoor Store, 323 Main Street, Red Wing, 612-388-5358

Northfield Public Library
210 Washington Street
Northfield, MN 55057

PART FOUR:
ROCHESTER AND
ITS NEIGHBORS

t

Rochester and Its Neighbors

In the geographic middle of southeastern Minnesota is a world-famous anomaly. The renowned Mayo Clinic, with its cutting-edge technology, is situated about 3 miles away from corn and soybean fields; the most sophisticated medical gear in the world abuts dairy farms and miles of prairies.

In these three rides you'll experience Rochester and its neighbors, in all their diversity, on foot and by bicycle. The lengths of these rides are short when compared with others in the book, but the time spent may not be. I recommend that you take your time to absorb it all. The Rochester area is truly one of a kind.

You might also want to think about combining any two of these three tours in a day's outing. In the summer, when the daylight lasts into late evening, a double-header is possible.

The rich diversity of this region is evident in these three rides. You pedal through downtown Rochester and its farm setting on your way to Mayowood. Or, you have the chance to stop for a picnic along a popular state bike trail, the Douglas State Trail, just north of town. Finally, in Tour 17 you can ride through one of America's greatest restored towns, Mantorville, and its nearby neighbors.

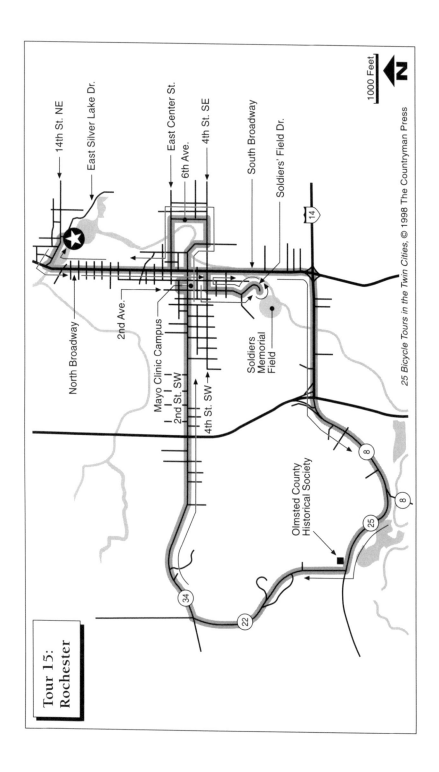

Tour 15: Rochester

14th St. NE

East Silver Lake Dr.

East Center St.

6th Ave.

4th St. SE

South Broadway

Soldiers' Field Dr.

North Broadway

2nd Ave.

Mayo Clinic Campus

2nd St. SW

4th St. SW

Soldiers Memorial Field

Olmsted County Historical Society

8

8

25

34

22

14

1000 Feet

N

25 Bicycle Tours in the Twin Cities, © 1998 The Countryman Press

15

Rochester

Distance: 14.1 miles
Terrain: Flat; active city traffic and quiet country roads
Location: Olmsted County
Special features: Mayo Medical Center, Civic Center, Soldiers Field,
Mayowood

Rochester is a natural for bicycle explorers. It embraces the great medical center and hospitals, it has remarkably diverse specialty shops, lots of parks and recreational areas, a fine civic center, art galleries, and more.

Beyond that, it has the famous Mayowood estate, the country home of the brothers Dr. Mayo. Tours are sponsored by the Olmsted County Historical Society (there is a fee). For information about the tour, call 507-282-9447. For Mayo Clinic tours, call 507-284-2315; for Methodist Hospital, call 507-286-7067; for St. Mary's Hospital, call 507-285-4507. You'll see the world-class medical technology without having to be a patient!

When in downtown Rochester, don't be surprised if you see people strolling about, mostly window-shopping, and wearing hospital-patient attire—slippers and robes. They are between tests, perhaps, with two hours between "chest X-ray" and "blood." This kind of street life is probably not seen in any other American city.

To park, from the city's major artery, North Broadway (also US 63), turn east onto 14th Street NE. After three blocks, find East Silver Lake Park Drive and park at the lot, which overlooks the lake. Other parking areas are available for bicyclists but this one is convenient and has the necessary facilities.

One of Rochester's many parks

0.0   *Ride north on East Silver Lake Drive. Turn left (west) onto 14th Street NE, and head for North Broadway.*

0.4   *Turn left (south) onto North Broadway and cross a bridge.*

The streets of Rochester are divided into four quadrants, which come together in the town's center. Thus, most of the street names in the downtown area include the directions NW, SW, NE, or SE.

0.8   *See the distinctive Mayo buildings on your right as you ride.*

1.5   *You are now in the center of Rochester, and North Broadway has become South Broadway. Turn right onto Second Street SW and ride one block west to First Avenue SW.*

If you wish to check out the Mayo Clinic, I recommended that you park and lock your bicycle here and walk, taking your time to explore.

1.7   *After riding another block west on Second Street SW, you'll come to Second Avenue SW.*

Here you'll find the Mayo Building. Take a right and walk to the center of it all. Mayo Clinic is at Third Avenue SW; another right turn takes you to Calvary Episcopal Church. Stroll around the block here.

2.0 *Continue to the Kahler Hotel, at First Avenue SW, and walk east back to Broadway with your bicycle. For all its widespread fame, Mayo Clinic is very compact.*

2.1 *Back where you started, head east on Second Street SW.*

2.2 *After three blocks, the street angles slightly south (right) to cross over a bridge. Now you are on Third Avenue SE.*

2.4 *Turn east (left) onto Fourth Street SE.*

2.5 *Turn left onto Sixth Avenue SE and ride to East Center Street. There turn left (west) and ride to the Civic Center.*

2.7 *Arrive at the Civic Center.*

The center contains the Civic Theatre, a large auditorium, and an art gallery. Again, you may want to lock up your bike at a nearby stand and walk around. This area is rightly the source of much pride. The gallery specializes in original modernism.

2.8 *Return to East Center Street and ride west.*

3.0 *Turn left onto South Broadway, toward Soldiers Memorial Field.*

4.0 *Turn right (west) onto Fourth Street SW, following the sign pointing to Soldiers Field.*

4.1 *Turn left (south) onto Second Avenue SW, and ride to the field.*

Look for the bicycle paths; find picnic tables, rest rooms, and water. This park, started in the 1930s, is a model of what civic leadership can achieve. It also has swimming, tennis, golf, and softball facilities.

4.6 *Retrace your route on Second Avenue SW and ride north. Turn right (east) onto Fourth Street SW.*

4.8 *Turn right (south) onto South Broadway.*

5.5 *Turn right onto US 14 and ride west toward Mayowood.*

Start looking for the signs pointing to CR 8.

6.2   Bear left (southeast) onto CR 8 at the sign saying BEGIN
        CR 8.

6.7   Bear right (northwest) onto CR 25.

*8.2   Turn right (north) at the sign for the Olmsted County
        Historical Society at the junction of CR 25 and CR 22.*

Park your bike at the society's parking lot. The tours for
Mayowood start here; a shuttle bus takes you to the estate.

*8.2   After your visit at the historical society, head north on CR 22,
        which starts at this junction.*

For miles now, you'll see some beautiful homes and farmland.

8.7   Turn right (east) onto CR 34 and continue into town.

*11.2   CR 34 turns into Second Street SW, which takes you past
        Saint Mary's Hospital. Continue on Second Street SW to
        South Broadway.*

*12.6   Turn left (north) onto South Broadway, and pedal back to your
        car at East Silver Lake Drive.*

Don't be surprised when you see West Silver Lake Drive
branching off Broadway. Don't turn here. Stay the course until
you reach 14th Street NE, and then turn right.

14.1   You arrive at the parking lot.

Bicycle Repair Service

Bicycle Sports, 1409 South Broadway, Rochester; 507-281-5007

16

Douglas State Trail

Distance: *26 miles*
Terrain: *Flat to gently rolling; no motorized traffic*
Location: *Olmsted and Goodhue Counties*
Special features: *Picnic grounds, rich farmlands, serenity*

The Douglas State Trail, which runs between Rochester and Pine Island, is as ideal a getaway ride as you could imagine. Almost all of it is flat; it passes through a rich mixture of farmland, woods, village, pasture, and prairie. You'll see an abundance of bird life, including a large number of partridge and the fabled Chinese ringneck pheasant. As a protected trail, it has no other vehicles on it, and the level terrain makes pedaling easy for younger cyclists. And if you forget to bring picnic supplies, or just on impulse pack up and go, you'll find a picnic supply store right on the trail!

This trail is accessible from two towns, Rochester and Pine Island, connected by US 52. From Rochester, go north on US 52, continuing past the intersection with US 14. Turn left (west) onto CR 4 and follow the signs to the Douglas Trail parking lot (you go by the IBM plant).

From Pine Island, drive south on US 52 to CR 11. You'll see the Douglas Trail signs directing you to the city park and the trailhead. Ample parking is available at both entrances, so this routing is reversible.

0.0 *Starting from Pine Island, you quickly find open country.*

This is some of the best farmland in Minnesota: the crops are bumper, the buildings are gleaming.

5.1 *Cross CR 3.*

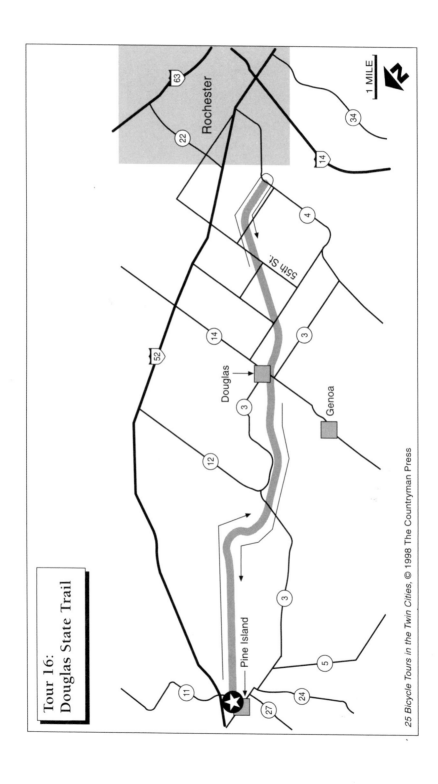

Tour 16:
Douglas State Trail

Rochester

Douglas

Genoa

Pine Island

55th St.

1 MILE

N

52

22

63

14

14

12

4

3

3

3

5

24

27

11

34

25 Bicycle Tours in the Twin Cities, © 1998 The Countryman Press

A farm outside Douglas

Here find a rest room and a shelter (in case of rain). Many small creeks meander through this area.

8.5 *Rest here at a full-service stop.*

It's picnic time. Fresh water, rest rooms, and picnic tables are available here. Within a quarter mile is the village of Douglas. There, the Trading Post has everything you need for a festive feast in the forest; food, paper products, and soda. On the next section of the ride you'll see more of the same wonderful scenery; open vistas with dairy cows waiting for their evening milking.

13.0 *You arrive near the IBM plant in Rochester. See the signs pointing to 55th Street NW and to Rochester. Now turn around and ride back on the Douglas State Trail to Pine Island and your car.*

26.0 *After a rewarding round-trip, you're back at your car.*

Bicycle Repair Service

Bicycle Sports, 1409 South Broadway, Rochester; 507-281-5007

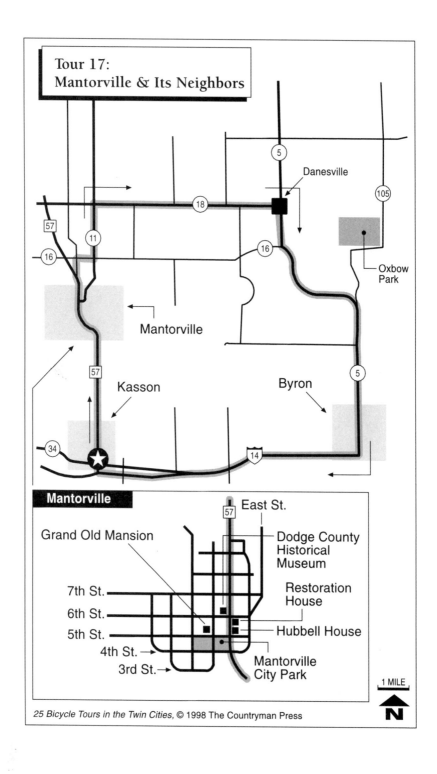

Tour 17:
Mantorville & Its Neighbors

5

Danesville

105

57

18

11

16

16

Oxbow
Park

Mantorville

57

Kasson

Byron

5

34

14

Mantorville

East St.

57

Grand Old Mansion

Dodge County
Historical
Museum

Restoration
House

7th St.

6th St.

Hubbell House

5th St.

4th St.

Mantorville
City Park

3rd St.

1 MILE

N

25 Bicycle Tours in the Twin Cities, © 1998 The Countryman Press

17

Mantorville and Its Neighbors

Distance: *22.4 miles*
Terrain: *Flat to gently rolling; small-town auto traffic*
Location: *Olmsted and Dodge Counties*
Special features: *Historic Mantorville, Oxbow Park, village charm*

Where else but in southeast Minnesota could you: (a) drive your car out of one of the world's great medical centers, (b) be within 30 minutes of a town that is totally dedicated to restored buildings, (c) pedal through farmlands, (d) tour a zoo park specializing in animal rehabilitation, and (e) realize you have not ridden more than 22-plus miles? The Mantorville loop is such a place. It belongs within the Rochester orbit of interesting and rewarding places to ride. Some folks might do both this tour and the Douglas State Trail (Tour 16) in one day.

Small-town charm is characteristic of this ride. From the parking lot in Kasson, a friendly and tidy village, you pedal to Mantorville. This is a most remarkable place—almost all of the buildings are on the National Register, having been carefully researched and rebuilt in the last 40 years. You'll find specialty shops, the county courthouse, and excellent restaurants and lodging at your fingertips. Then the loop takes you out into open country, with well-managed farms prevailing.

Serendipity pops up at a truly wondrous small zoo, Oxbow County Park (507-775-2451). It embraces 12 miles of cross-country trails for hiking and some 572 acres of hardwood forest, meadows, and bluffs. Its nature center experts care for about 30 species of Minnesota wildlife, including bison, cougars, otters, wolves, and birds of prey. All have either been injured, taken inappropriately from the wild, or are overstocks from other zoos. No admission is charged, but donations are welcome. Then on the last leg of the loop, you come to Byron, as straight out of Norman Rockwell's America as any place could be. All this in a little over 20 miles.

To park, take US 14 west from Rochester. At MN 57, 14 miles from the Rochester city limits, turn right (north) and drive to Kasson. Park on Main Street.

0.0   *Ride north on MN 57 to Mantorville.*

2.8   *Arrive in Mantorville by crossing over the Zumbro River.*

This is one of the major drainage systems of southeastern Minnesota.

Lock your bicycle and stroll around town. A good starting point is the carefully prepared map (in bronze) of the entire community mounted at the Hubbell House, on the corner of Main and Fifth Streets. This map shows the extent of the restoration, as well as showing the shops selling homemade goodies, hand-crafted arts and furniture, and general merchandise. Yet Mantorville doesn't have the feeling of a tourist trap; the items are of high quality, and the sales pressure is nonexistent.

Throughout the village are several wonderful churches more than a century old. You'll also see the Opera House, which presents live musicals on summer weekends; an excellent county historical museum; and several bed & breakfasts. Just at the north end of town is the courthouse, restored with faithful attention to its original design.

3.3   *Head north on MN 57, also called Main Street.*

3.6   *Turn left (north) onto CR 11.*

You will cross CR 16; stay on CR 11.

5.2   *Turn right (east) onto CR 18.*

Here is choice farmland with huge Harvestore silos, tall trees, and well-kept grain fields. Look for the Furst Brothers Dairy Farm.

6.4   *Here on the left is an unusual sight, a green-brick barn.*

Note the abundance of wildflowers in the ditches. How did they get there? Prepare for some hills coming soon; remember, they always look much steeper from far away than they really are. Once you get there, they seem tame.

9.9 *Turn right (south) onto CR 5.*

The downhill work starts here. You'll cross CR 16 again, but continue south on CR 5.

11.2 *Turn left onto CR 105.*

See the signs pointing to Oxbow Park, one mile north from the intersection on CR 105. It's an easy ride to the park. When ready, make a U-turn and ride back to CR 5.

13.2 *Back on CR 5, ride south to Byron, the last destination.*

16.4 *Arrive in Byron.*

In town, note the water tower, looking like nothing so much as the outfit worn by the Tin Man in *The Wizard of Oz.* See Byron's modern tower also, on the left. Note the immaculate, picture-postcard town image.

17.2 *Turn right (west) onto US 14, and ride back to Kasson.*

Caution: This is an active highway with four lanes. (CR 34 follows the same general route, but stay on US 14.)

22.4 *Arrive in Kasson and your car.*

Bicycle Repair Service

The nearest repair service is found 14 miles east of Kasson:

Bicycle Sports, 1409 South Broadway, Rochester; 507-281-5007

PART FIVE:
FIVE OF A KIND

Five of a Kind

Bicycling gives the rider a sense of the daily lives and dwellings of other people. You can pedal along easily, noting those features that impart a distinctive ambience to a locale: gardens, mailboxes, lawn art, playground equipment, domestic and commercial architecture. All these are instantly accessible to the rider.

These features, in Part Five, are located on terrain that is generally flat to gently rolling. A few steep hills are to be found, but mostly the land is easily tourable. Often you will find very flat, very open areas inviting a kind of solitude that can renew the spirit. Each tour goes through at least one town; all of them, including my hometown, are very friendly.

Each town also takes great pride in accenting those historical, aesthetic, and natural features that create its identity. A friendly rivalry emerges with nearby towns, the results of which are at the fingertips of the rider. These next five rides all bring the cyclist into that world. Look for both the distinctive and the shared qualities of these five of a kind.

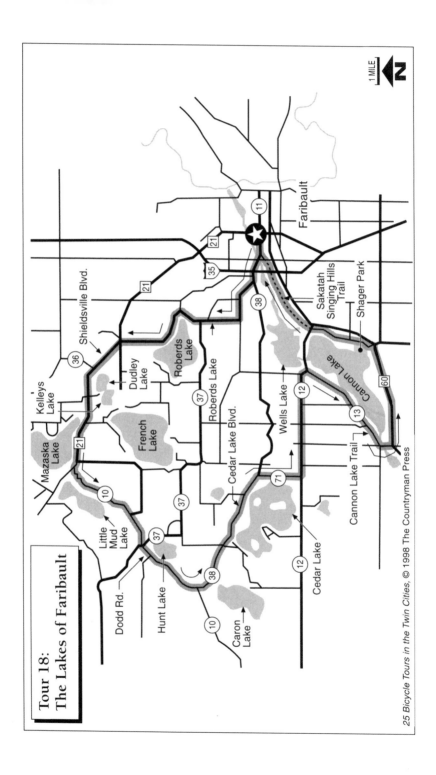

Tour 18:
The Lakes of Faribault

25 Bicycle Tours in the Twin Cities, © 1998 The Countryman Press

18

The Lakes of Faribault

Distance: *33.1 miles*
Terrain: *Flat to gently rolling; light automotive traffic*
Location: *Rice County*
Special features: *The lakes, St. Patrick's Catholic Church*

Every reader of license plates knows that the blue, green, and white plates of Minnesota proclaim it the "Land of 10,000 Lakes." Actually, more than 11,500 have been identified, but the number 10,000 is accepted as fact. Many are sources of great pride among Gopher State residents, providing recreation, hospitality, and income. Beyond that, during the long, cold months of winter, Minnesotans have the assurance that the days of fishing, swimming, and boating will soon supplant the weeks of waiting for the snow to melt.

This tour takes us to 10 lakes and many eye-catching views. Faribault itself has an interesting history, reaching back into the fur-trading days of the 1830s, expanding under the leadership of Episcopal Bishop Henry Whipple into a private school mecca (Shattuck School, St. Mary's School), and standing today as a bustling city of some 20,000, many of whom live at least part-time on one of the lakes. Riders can learn more about that history by stopping at the chamber of commerce, located only 0.1 mile from the tour's takeoff point.

To park, exit I-35 at exit 59 and go east on MN 21. Find the junction of MN 21 and CR 11. Park at either the Burger King or the Golden Corral restaurant.

0.0 *Head northwest on CR 11. This is also known as Seventh Street.*

0.1 Find the chamber of commerce.

The chamber offers several self-guided tours of the nearby community.

0.2 Pass Sakatah Singing Hills Bicycle Trail.

Remember this, as you will be returning on that trail. Note the marinas and tackle shops; this is lake country.

1.2 Turn right to continue on CR 11 (here also known as Roberds Lake Boulevard).

Note how close the road is to the shore of Roberds Lake.

3.7 Riding along the boulevard, note the public facilities available.

The crowning beauty of the area is its stands of trees—old, new, of many varieties, all shading the year-round residents.

4.3 Turn left (northwest) onto CR 21, also known as Shieldsville Boulevard.

5.0 The boulevard takes you out into farmland.

People hang out their wash and tend their gardens; you are riding up close to it all.

5.3 See the second and third lakes of this tour, Kellys Lake and Dudley Lake, behind the heavy shoreline foliage.

These lakes are not publicly appealing; they serve as drainage basins.

6.8 Pass—but do not take—the turnoff for French Lake.

8.8 Arrive at Mazaska Lake, which has public access.

9.4 Turn left onto CR 10 (also known as Dodd Road), which leads to Shieldsville.

As you turn, note appropriately named Little Mud Lake on your right. Rest rooms, public telephones, and food are available along CR 10.

10.2 Arrive at a tour highlight, St. Patrick's Catholic Church.

St. Patrick's has been ministering for the last 80 years, and is usually open to visitors. If you're ready for a break, drop in, then tour the cemetery.

Serenity at Wells Lake

10.5 *Return to CR 10.*

This section of the road dips and rises rhythmically.

13.1 *You're at Foxhill Apple Orchard.*

Stop for a sample. Nearby is Hunt Lake, small but clean.

14.6 *Turn left onto CR 38, also called Cedar Lake Boulevard.*

Observe Caron Lake with new residences and impressive trees.

17.1 *Arrive at Cedar Lake.*

Cedar Lake is the heart of Faribault lake country. It has islands and a lively resort business.

17.4 *Turn right onto CR 71.*

Note the beautiful homes.

19.7 *Turn left (east) onto CR 12, a major artery where the auto traffic increases.*

20.6 *Note the wonderful redbrick building, circa 1890.*

22.8 *Turn right (south) onto CR 13 (Cannon Lake Trail).*

CR 13 leads to Wells Lake and Cannon Lake. Be ready for beautiful scenery.

25.9 *Note the Channel Inn.*

26.1 *CR 13 bears south here. Turn left (east) onto MN 60.*

The road has busy traffic but good shoulders.

28.9 *Turn left at the sign into Shager Park, and come to the Sakatah Singing Hills Trail, operated by the State of Minnesota. Turn right onto the trail and ride back to Faribault.*

Along the way note the large size and the watercraft of Cannon Lake. See Wells Lake as the signs indicate.

33.1 *You arrive at your car.*

Treat yourself to a meal; several eateries are nearby.

Bicycle Repair Service

Village Pedaler, 311 Central Avenue, Faribault, 507-332-2636

19

Northfield and Faribault

Distance: *47.6 miles*
Terrain: *Flat to moderately hilly; light automotive traffic*
Location: *Rice County*
Special features: *First National Bank Museum, historic buildings in*
Faribault

This route is extremely rich in local history and scenery, outstanding agriculture, and ethnic heritage. You ride through two cities, each with much to offer. Northfield annually sponsors the Defeat of Jesse James Days, a five-day celebration of the first time that citizens actually stopped the most notorious bank-robbing gang of the day. Northfield also serves as a major center for agricultural production and is the national home of MaltoMeal cereals. It has two famous liberal arts colleges, Carleton and St. Olaf, and was the hometown of two world-famous authors, Ole E. Rolvaag (*Giants in the Earth*) and Thorstein Veblen (*The Theory of the Leisure Class*). Faribault, meanwhile (see also Tour 18), has nurseries, parks, and restored buildings worth careful attention.

Northfield is shaped by its economy, its schools, and its heritage. The tour will follow, as closely as possible, the roads on which the James gang entered and fled from the city. Some creative reconstruction is needed, of course, because the gang's exact departure route was not recorded.

Some historical detail is needed at this point. The gang, eight in all, known by 1876 nationally as the most fearsome of all bank robbers, decided to strike in the Upper Midwest. From their homes in Missouri, they traveled to St. Paul, dividing into two groups of four. One band reconnoitered Red Wing, then came to Northfield. The other looked at

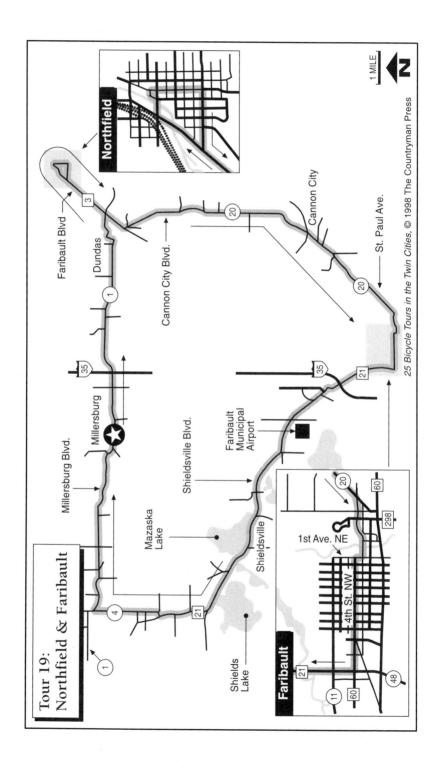

Tour 19:
Northfield & Faribault

Northfield

Faribault

1 MILE

N

25 Bicycle Tours in the Twin Cities, © 1998 The Countryman Press

Faribault Blvd

Dundas

Cannon City Blvd.

Cannon City

St. Paul Ave.

Millersburg

Millersburg Blvd.

Mazaska Lake

Shieldsville Blvd.

Faribault Municipal Airport

Shieldsville

Shields Lake

1st Ave. NE

4th St. NW

3

20

20

1

35

35

21

20

60

298

21

11

60

48

4

21

1

Mankato for a robbery. They joined up in Mankato and decided on Northfield. On September 6 they divided up again with half staying the night in Millersburg (where your tour begins) and the other in Cannon City.

The James gang didn't know that First National Bank officials had been told by informants that a raid would probably take place there, on the 7th. The staff and police were, in fact, awaiting their Missouri visitors. After considerable exchange of gunfire and general mayhem, two Northfielders and two gang members were killed; the remainder of the robbers fled westward beyond reach. As you look at the map, note that the gang came in from two different directions and rode out by a third.

This proved to be a major turning point in American criminal history: The days of small-town bank robbery were over.

Be sure to see the splendid Northfield Historical Society Museum, at 408 South Division Street (507-645-9268); a fee is charged. You might also want to see MaltoMeal, directly across the Cannon River from the museum. Also nearby are the two schools in this, as its residents call it, "the city of cows, colleges, and contentment."

To park, take I-35 from the Twin Cities (or from the south) to exit 66. From there, turn west onto CR 1 and drive 1.7 miles to Millersburg. Park at the Blue Horse Saloon. See the small building nearby where half the James gang slept on September 6, 1876.

0.0 *Ride east from Millersburg on CR 1 (also called Millersburg Boulevard), retracing the way you drove in. At the Interstate exit, continue on CR 1.*

You pass some great farms here.

2.5 *Note the Schroeder place on your left, where high-tech agriculture is on display.*

4.1 *You go through a farm, with the house on one side of the road, and the farm buildings on the other.*

5.7 *Enter Dundas, with its stately trees.*

6.2 *Cross the railroad tracks, remembering that the James gang came on horseback, not by railroad train.*

6.3 *In downtown Dundas, turn left (north) onto CR 1.*

6.9 *At a stop sign, note the graceful All Souls Episcopal Church.*

ERLING JORSTAD

The James gang was defeated here.

7.1 *Turn left (north) onto MN 3 (Faribault Boulevard).*

8.3 *Note, on your left, the Jesse James Bowling Lanes.*

9.4 *Find Riverside Park, on your right, with water, picnic tables, and rest rooms.*

9.8 *At the traffic light, turn right onto Fifth Street, cross the Cannon River, and then turn left onto Water Street.*

10.0 *Ride one block north on Water Street, then turn right just after the post office and ride one more block east to the First National Bank Museum.*

This museum is part of the Northfield Historical Society's museum. The raid occurred here. Knowledgeable volunteer guides are ready to answer questions. In front, the raid is reenacted during the Defeat of Jesse James Days festival in early September.

10.1 *Ride south on Division Street. The defeated gang rode this way out, having lost two members and looking for Mankato.*

10.5 *Turn right (west) onto Woodley Street, also known as 10th Street.*

10.8 *At the stop light, turn left (west) onto MN 3.*

12.5 *Turn left (south) onto CR 20 (Cannon City Boulevard), headed for Cannon City.*

You encounter a hefty hill here, with good shoulders.

14.3 *Note the dwelling built into the hill on your left, known hereabouts as an "energy house."*

You are out of Northfield and into superb farm land.

19.5 *Enter Cannon City.*

You'll ride by immaculate homes, but alas there are no facilities.

21.2 *Pass the Nauman Farm on your right.*

Note the restored buildings (including an original town hall), gorgeous flowers, and sturdy barns.

22.3 *Find the first nurseries and orchards for which Faribault is famous. More to come.*

24.1 *Turn right onto Ravine Street, and ride a hilly road into Faribault.*

Perhaps the James gang came this way, no doubt keeping to the outskirts of Faribault.

24.5 *See the Straight River, and the depot, now a café.*

24.7 *Turn right (north) onto First Avenue NE, and ride on it for one block.*

24.8 *Turn left (west) onto Fourth Street NW, also known as MN 60, and see the post office.*

In short order, you'll pass the Rice County Court House, built with local limestone, and the historic Farmer Seed and Nursery business.

26.0 *Turn right (north) onto CR 21 (also known as Shieldsville Boulevard), at the Kentucky Fried Chicken location. Continue on, crossing CR 11 and I-35.*

28.1 *Still on MN 21, turn left (northwest) and soon find open country.*

28.4 *See the Airtech Park and Faribault Municipal Airport.*

33.1 *Here you are truly in Faribault lake country (also see Tour 18).*

33.7 *Arrive at Mazaska Lake and the town of Shieldsville.*

Public facilities are available. Some of the James gang rode here en route to Northfield.

36.4 *Find a good roadbed, along with beautiful agricultural scenery.*

37.3 *Turn right (north) onto CR 4.*

43.1 *Turn right (east) onto CR 1.*

This is also known as Millersburg Boulevard.

47.6 *You are back at the Blue Horse Saloon and your car.*

Bicycle Repair Service

Mike's Bicycle Shop2, 415½ Division Street South, Northfield; 507-645-9452

20

Kenyon

Distance: *37.9 miles*
Terrain: *Flat to moderately rolling; quiet country roads*
Location: *Goodhue, Rice, and Steele Counties*
Special features: *Rose Boulevard, upscale farms, threshing machines*

Each town showcases its unique features. Kenyon and environs have several: a wonderful four-block boulevard on Main Street with dozens of carefully tended rosebushes; churches; a well-kept business area; a progressive public school; and the historic Gunderson House, built in 1895 in Queen Anne style. The town has undergone profound changes; some small businesses have fallen due to Wal-Mart, 800 numbers and mail-order, interstate highways, and national credit cards. But the 1598 Kenyonites have adapted, and Kenyon's small-town ambience continues to revolve around its schools, its commerce, and its loyalty to its Norwegian heritage (see also Tour 23).

Drive into Kenyon and find Main Street at the junction of MN 56 and MN 60. Park here (there are no parking meters).

0.0 *Point your bicycle westward on Main Street, which becomes Gunderson Boulevard.*

Enjoy the roses in summer; many have been planted as memorials.

0.3 *Find the Gunderson House on your left.*

0.4 *Turn left (south) onto CR 12, also known as Huseth Street.*

0.6 *See Great Lakes Hybrids, a high-technology company.*

Some bumps are to be found on the roadway here, but they help

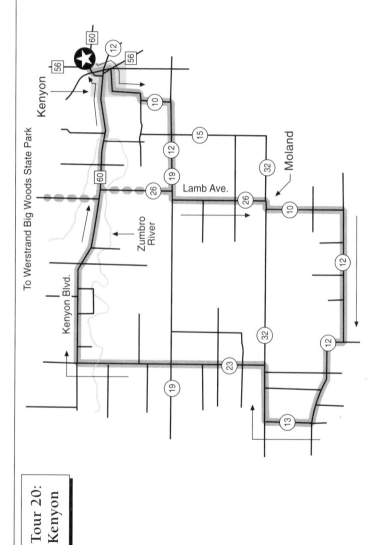

**Tour 20:
Kenyon**

Kenyon

To Werstrand Big Woods State Park

Kenyon Blvd.

Zumbro
River

Lamb Ave.

Moland

1 MILE

N

keep you alert. Note the 90-degree angles along this road, unusual in modern highway construction.

5.1 *Note the sign, in a rural area, for licensed day care.*

The "new family" has come to the farm country!

5.7 *See the sign for Nerstrand Big Woods State Park.*

This is a pleasant facility noted for its extensive stand of virgin timber. It is 8.1 miles north from this point, and it makes a nice side trip.

5.8 *Ride left (south) onto CR 26, also known as Lamb Avenue.*

6.9 *See the isolated elm tree; what would explain its solitude?*

8.9 *Turn right (west) onto CR 32 for 0.3 mile.*

Note, just to the left, an old creamery known as Moland. It is not in use anymore.

9.2 *Turn left (south) onto CR 10.*

10.3 *Find Moland Lutheran Church.*

This church was founded by Rev. B.J. Muus, a Norwegian minister who planted many churches in Minnesota. The parsonage is next door.

10.9 *Find interesting yard art.*

Note the grassy shoulders.

11.7 *As CR 10 ends, turn right (west) onto CR 12. Here is high-tech agriculture on display; modern equipment allows farms to be as large as 800 acres.*

15.9 *CR 12 bends slightly to the right and goes past the restored Merton Township Hall.*

This and similar buildings are still used by residents for considering issues such as roads, bridges, schools, and agricultural innovations including large animal feedlots. This carries on the tradition envisioned by Thomas Jefferson, the creator of the township system of governance.

19.2 *Turn right (north) onto CR 13, and follow it as it turns right (east).*

22.5 *Turn left (north) onto CR 23.*

ERLING JORSTAD

Those great old threshing machines

24.6 *Here is a fine long-distance vista of the old and the new: old farmhouses and new farm machinery and farm buildings.*

28.8 *Turn right (east) onto MN 60.*

The highway is freshly resurfaced and excellent for bicycles.

30.8 *Serendipity appears. Find a collection of more than 20 threshing machines.*

Also known as grain separators, these machines have been replaced by high-tech combines, and are now symbols of a long-gone but favored past. The owner has ringed his farm with them, quite possibly the only such collection in the Upper Midwest. These were the machines for the neighborhood rings as immortalized in Grant Wood's painting *The Threshers*. Today they evoke nostalgia for the old days. The trees in midsummer bloom provide shade over some of the machines.

31.2 *See the Prairieville United Methodist Church.*

36.8 *Pass Gol Lutheran Church, carefully built of stone. This church, too, was founded by The Reverend B.J. Muus.*

37.0 Ride over a bridge spanning the Zumbro River.

37.9 You are at Gunderson Boulevard and your car. Find restaurants and facilities in town.

Bicycle Repair Service

The nearest service is 14 miles west of Kenyon:

Village Pedaler, 311 Central Avenue, Faribault; 507-332-2636

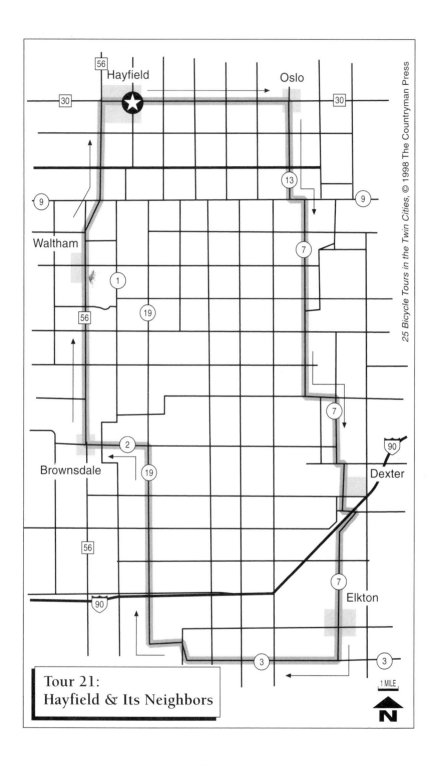

25 Bicycle Tours in the Twin Cities, © 1998 The Countryman Press

Tour 21:
Hayfield & Its Neighbors

Hayfield

Oslo

Waltham

Brownsdale

Dexter

Elkton

1 MILE

N

21

Hayfield and Its Neighbors

Distance: *58.4 miles*
Terrain: *Flat to gently rolling; light rural traffic*
Location: *Dodge and Mower Counties*
Special features: *The charms of four small towns, high-tech farming, open country*

Hayfield's town motto is well chosen: "Where People Make Progress." As technology and world market conditions remade old-time farming, people here (and in the other villages on the trail) adapted smoothly to the pressures for change. Hayfield, the largest town on today's tour, reflects the area's evolution over these years: it features both older houses and snazzy farm equipment, traditional yard art and up-to-date schools. The other three towns, although near the commercial lures of I-90, have also retained their identities. They offer hospitality for the rider on this long, flatland excursion.

To park, locate Hayfield near the junction of MN 56 and MN 30. Enter town on MN 30, and head for the water tower at the intersection of Main and Center Streets. A block east, on Main Street, you can locate the largest church, Trinity Lutheran. Park on Main Street; it isn't metered.

0.0 Start by riding north on Center Street.

0.2 Turn right (east) onto MN 30.

There's a fine city park here, with facilities.

3.9 You are in the wide open country.

Note the sign pointing to Oslo, suggesting the ethnic heritage of the founders.

Tractors in Oslo

5.5   *Arrive in Oslo.*
See the country store, which features lutefisk for sale. The Farmall tractors—true cultural artifacts—are also of note here.

5.6   *Turn right (south) onto CR 13.*

6.0   *Find Vernon Township Hall, well preserved.*

6.5   *A farm painted all in white is a landmark here.*
Farther along is a classic blend of old and new farm buildings.

9.6   *Bear slightly left at Evanger Lutheran Church.*

12.3   *Here CR 13 becomes CR 7. Continue south on CR 7.*

19.0   *You are entering Dexter, the first of three satellite villages.*
Dexter has its charms, with its tidy homes and facilities for riders.

20.3   *Cross over I-90, through an area with restaurants and gas stations. Stay on CR 7 south, noting a small airport. Just before*

reaching Elkton, you ride on both CR 7 and CR 2 for a quarter mile. Stay on CR 7.

28.4 *Enter Elkton.*

This is a lovely town for those who want privacy yet wish to be near larger cities via the interstate. Elkton has all facilities. A landmark is a traditional water tower.

32.7 *Turn right (west) onto CR 3.*

37.7 *Turn right (north) onto CR 19.*

40.5 *You ride over I-90 again.*

47.7 *Turn left (west) onto CR 2.*

You arrive in Brownsdale.

48.1 *Turn right (north) onto MN 56.*

This is a wonderful road for cycling, with great farm views.

58.2 *Turn right (east) onto MN 30.*

58.4 *You're back in Hayfield, where you'll find eateries and facilities.*

Bicycle Repair Service

The nearest service is 22 miles east of Hayfield:

Bicycle Sports, 1409 South Broadway, Rochester, 507-281-5007

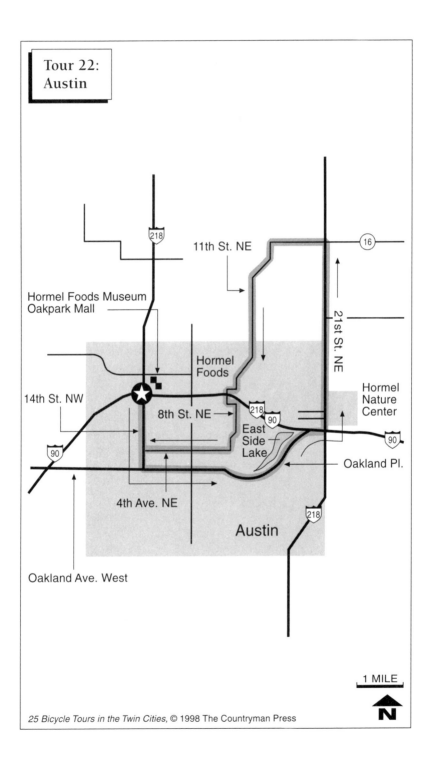

Tour 22:
Austin

11th St. NE

Hormel Foods Museum
Oakpark Mall

Hormel
Foods

14th St. NW

8th St. NE

East
Side
Lake

21st St. NE

Hormel
Nature
Center

Oakland Pl.

4th Ave. NE

Austin

Oakland Ave. West

1 MILE

N

25 Bicycle Tours in the Twin Cities, © 1998 The Countryman Press

22

Austin

Distance: 14.2 miles
Terrain: Flat; moderate city traffic
Location: Mower County
Special features: SPAMorama, Jay Hormel Nature Center

To pedal through Austin (Spamtown, USA) is to discover a blend of agri-culture, livestock husbandry, high-tech food production, and Madison Avenue promotion. The town zestfully identifies with the Hormel Food Company, manufacturer of, among other things, Little Sizzlers, Wranglers, Dinty Moore, and Spam. The growth of this food empire over the decades has moved Hormel into the ranks of Fortune 500 compa-nies. Its promotion of Spam as a staple in the American military diet of World War II gave it an international recognition it promotes to this day.

The retail stores of Austin carry all manner of Spam memorabilia: baseball caps, T-shirts, jackets, and ashtrays. On the city's main street, banners on the light poles proclaim SPAMTOWN, USA or SPAMTOWN, MIN-NESOTA. The high school nickname is the Packers. Austin's most famous mansion and its nature center are named for the founding Hormel family.

Spam is indeed an American cultural artifact; given its name from "spiced ham," this canned meat is the joy of fast-food aficionados and the bane of health food devotees. It is simple to prepare (some like it chilled); it goes well with a variety of condiments (including salsa and green peas), and it is easily storable. It is, well—like nothing else on the market.

The city and its environs offer the rider a rewarding look at how this town has endured the many fluctuations of agricultural production, adapted to changing traffic and housing patterns, maintained a strong downtown retail presence despite the lure of suburban malls, and provided educational opportunities with both a community and a technical college.

This tour takes you through much of Austin, not just the Hormel empire. It is a slice of life in a town proud of its heritage, happy to celebrate its icon with a four-day Spamjam festival. The tour is rather short, but it's designed to allow time to sample the full flavor at your own pace.

To park, heading east on I-90, take exit 177 north. This takes you to US 218. Drive north on that a block and find OakPark Mall. Enter the mall and find Younkers Department Store at the far west end. Park your car there. Leave your bicycle in your automobile. At the mall, find the east side entrance and walk down a long corridor into the atrium. You'll find the Hormel Museum on your right as you enter the atrium. Full of nostalgic memorabilia, it's a great introduction to your upcoming ride.

0.0 *Ride out of OakPark Mall and turn left (south) onto US 218, also known as 14th Street NW. You are headed for Oakland Avenue West, also known as Business I-90, as noted on green signs.*

2.1 *Here you turn left (east) onto Oakland Avenue West, the city's major artery.*

Traffic is brisk but the street is wide.

3.1 *Pass Austin Morning Lions Club park, with facilities if you need them.*

3.5 *Arrive at the scenic part of downtown Austin. Oakland Avenue West becomes Oakland Place headed northeasterly.*

You go by East Side Lake. Notice the SPAMTOWN banners along Oakland Place.

4.4 *Take a right onto I-90, with its wide lanes.*

You are very briefly on I-90, but very safe.

4.5 *Take exit 180-B and head north onto 21st Street NE (CR 21).*

4.8 *Note the great yard art at the home on your left.*

5.0 *Arrive at the entrance to the Jay Hormel Nature Center.*

Plan to spend time here on foot. The center was created by matching funds from public and private sources. It has handsome exhibits of local aquatic wildlife, deer, and other animals; 6 miles of walking trails over 278 wooded acres; an auditorium for programs by local naturalists; and all facilities., including security areas for bicycles. The center is ideal for both family outings and solo communes with nature. A donation is appreciated. For more information, call 507-437-7519.

5.1 *Turn right (north) onto 21st Street NE again.*

Ride along wonderful farmland on flat terrain.

7.3 *At the stop sign, turn left (west) onto CR 16.*

9.6 *Turn left (south) onto 11th Street NE.*

10.1 *Turn right (southwest) onto Eighth Street NE.*

19.4 *Arrive at the Hormel empire headquarters, the Research Institute (for agricultural products), and the Hormel Food corporate office, the nerve center for this conglomerate.*

10.6 *Continue on Eighth Street NE headed south.*

10.9 *Turn right (west) onto Fourth Avenue NE.*

11.8 *Turn right (north) onto 14th Street NW.*

14.1 *Cross I-90 and find US 218 again (which is also 14th Street NW).*

14.2 *You are now back at the mall. Hungry?*

Find a retail store for *Spam-what-am*!

Bicycle Repair Service

Rydjor Bike Shop, 219 North Main, Austin; 507-433-7571 or 1-800-575-7571

PART SIX:
ETHNIC HERITAGE

Ethnic Heritage

The world of ethnic heritage and religious identity in southeast Minnesota offers bicyclists an opportunity to extend their understanding of a basic ingredient of the area's life. With these three rides, we look directly at how the immigrants understood why they had come to America; what it would take for them to survive—even flourish—here; and what their vision of the future was for their children.

I focus here on three groups and the physical expression of their commitment as it took form in their churches. These structures are material statements of what the people believed and how they felt they should conduct their lives. Each tour in this section takes a look at the ethnic community surrounding one cathedral-like building, the mother church for that particular region.

By observing the farms planted, the towns built, and the churches nurtured in this region, we see how their builders understood the American dream. As underclass immigrants, they hoped to make a fresh start in the new world through land ownership, education for their children, and freedom to pursue their religious beliefs.

Most of the churches were started in the countryside, where many remain. They became centers for worship, for education in the faith (and sometimes in the English language), for socialization with the neighbors, for courtship, and for business. They embraced the life cycle: baptism, confirmation, marriage, and burial. Their excellent physical condition today is a testament to the commitment of their congregations.

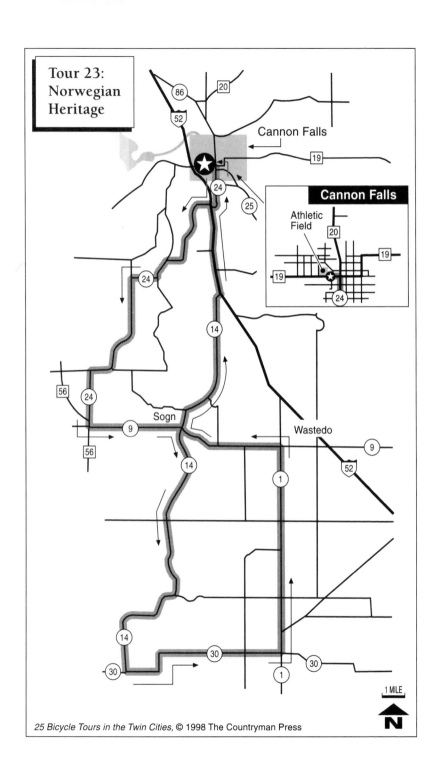

Tour 23:
Norwegian
Heritage

Cannon Falls

Cannon Falls

Athletic
Field

Sogn

Wastedo

1 MILE

N

25 Bicycle Tours in the Twin Cities, © 1998 The Countryman Press

23

Norwegian Heritage

Distance: *42.7 miles*
Terrain: *Flat to manageably hilly; light, rural traffic*
Location: *Goodhue County*
Special features: *Ethnic churches, lovely farms, Sogn Valley*

Among the first permanent European settlers in the Upper Midwest were
the Norwegian immigrants, some arriving in the 1820s. By the middle of
that century, substantial numbers were moving out to the rich farmlands
of southern Minnesota. The first settlers in Goodhue County came in the
1850s, arriving in 1854 at what they would call Holden Church and
claiming the land.

That church was the first Norwegian Lutheran congregation for many
miles around. Its first pastor, Rev. B.J. Muus, and his family arrived from
Norway in 1859. Within a few years a building was erected and the new
community expanded in numbers. Muus served as a church planter,
traveling far north and west to baptize, confirm, marry, and bury fellow
Norse Lutherans. From the springboard of Holden, seven similar congregations were started in the next 20 years. Wondrously maintained to
this day, Holden is the mother church for this ethnic group.

While you're there, take time to look through the graveyard, which
has many stories to tell. It shows that in the 19th century the women
generally died much younger than the men, many of them in childbirth.
There were many stillborn or early infant mortalities, and by the 1920s
the inscriptions on the tombstones were changing from Norse to English,
a sure sign of immigrant acculturation. Note the heavily ethnic flavor of
many of the names; today one rarely finds such appellations as "Olaus"
and "Borghild." Finally, when on the inside of these churches, note the

stained-glass windows, which illustrate symbols of faith. The church architecture of the three groups covered in this section—Norse, Swede, and Slavic—is emblematic of the "high church" style: it is stately, set apart from everyday life, and elaborate; features include pipe organs, and the cross and altar at the center.

To park, go to Cannon Falls and find the downtown intersection of MN 19, MN 20, and CR 24. This intersection is 0.5 mile east of US 52 (Cannon Falls exit). One block west of the intersection you'll find the parking lot, which is also the lot for the Cannon Valley Trail (see Tour 2).

0.0 *From the parking lot turn left (east) and ride to the stoplight. There turn right (south) onto CR 24 and ride through town.*

1.1 *At Cannon Mall, CR 24 turns right. Continue on it, crossing US 52.*

1.4 *Find open country, stretching west and south.*

You pass by one of Cannon Falls' several horse ranches.

2.5 *Ride up a pretty hill, the first of several more ahead.*

5.8 *Come to the first Norwegian Lutheran church, this one named Wangen Prairie.*

This is one of the eight churches founded by the Reverend Mr. Muus; it still flourishes.

5.9 *Prepare for another substantial hill.*

Your reward is the great view at the top.

9.5 *Here is a textbook farm: a classic red barn and white farmhouse on your right.*

9.9 *At the junction of CR 24 with MN 56 and CR 9, ride left (east) onto CR 9.*

This takes you to Sogn Valley.

11.5 *Prepare for a long descent, which finally levels off at 12.4 miles.*

This brings you to the hamlet of Sogn (no facilities).

12.7 *Turn right (south) onto CR 14.*

This is the southern half of Sogn Valley (you ride the northern half later during this tour). It has manageable hills. Notice how few residences are for sale. The houses are immaculately clean and the lawns beautifully manicured. In good weather, the wash is hung out to dry in this bucolic valley.

14.9 *Some of these farms have been in the same family for three generations, such as the Maring place just here on your left.*

17.6 *The showcase residence here was built by the area distributor of Harvestores, those huge blue silos.*

18.5 *Stay with this hill for another great topside vista.*

This is some of the best farmland in America.

18.8 *Note the heliport; high-tech comes to the immigrant valley.*

21.1 *Turn left (east) onto CR 30.*

You see an abandoned one-room school house, named Dovre.

23.4 *This is the beginning of the original 860-acre homestead owned by my great-grandfather. It was later divided for his sons and son-in-law. He gave a portion of the estate to Holden Church in the 1860s; the first and subsequent buildings were erected there.*

23.7 *The original homestead is on your left (north).*

Stephanie Edwards, the anchor personality of Channel 7 in Los Angeles, grew up here. The American Dream came true in a way unknown to my ancestors. She is my cousin.

24.4 *See the parsonage on the left and, next to it, Holden Community Park.*

The park building you see here was once a depot in Wanamingo, and was brought here by Holdenites; the park itself is a delight.

24.7 *Arrive at Holden Church.*

This church and its graveyard are worth a walk around and through. Note the monument to the Reverend B.J. Muus at the entry.

24.8 *Head east on CR 30. Turn left (north) onto CR 1.*

26.0 *Arrive at Aspelund (named for a town in Norway) Lutheran Church.*

This is also Norwegian Lutheran, but separate in governance from the others on this tour.

ERLING JORSTAD

Holden Church

26.1 Head north on CR 1.

Watch for the rise and fall of the road. Observe the crops being harvested; in a good season a farmer can bring in four crops of hay from these rich fields.

29.6 Ride left (west) onto CR 9.

32.5 Find Urland Lutheran Church, also named for a place in Norway.

Compare its architecture, graveyard, and interior to the other three churches on this tour.

32.5 Return to CR 9 and head west.

34.8 In Sogn, turn right (north) onto CR 14 and ride into my favorite valley in America!

This one speaks for itself with the soft roll of the hills, the virgin woods, the inviting lawns and wandering creeks. It brings to mind the countryside of southern England.

34.8 CR 14 ends here; turn right and ride to US 52. Turn left onto US 52 and ride north.

The road is busy, but there are four lanes, and it's a pleasant ride back to Cannon Falls.

41.0 *Turn right onto CR 24 and follow it north.*

42.7 *You're back in downtown Cannon Falls and at your car.*

Bicycle Repair Service

Trail Station Sports, 106 Fourth Street North, Cannon Falls; 507-263-5055 or 1-888-835-BIKE

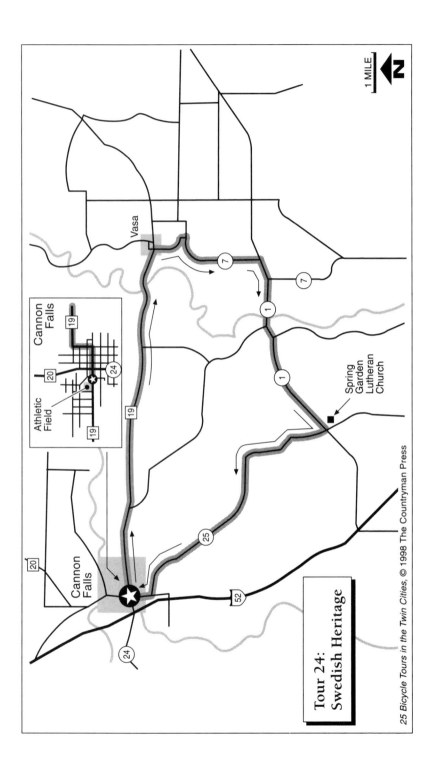

Vasa

7

7

1

1

Spring Garden Lutheran Church

25

52

24

20

Cannon Falls

Cannon Falls

19

20

24

19

Athletic Field

1 MILE

N

Tour 24: Swedish Heritage

25 Bicycle Tours in the Twin Cities, © 1998 The Countryman Press

24

Swedish Heritage

Distance: *28.2 miles*
Terrain: *Flat to moderately hilly; light rural traffic*
Location: *Goodhue County*
Special features: *Three churches, great farms, open spaces*

Touring the land of Swedish heritage turns into a fine opportunity to see traditional churches and the scenery of southeast Minnesota at its best. The first Swedish settlers arrived here in 1853, settled near Vasa, and claimed the unbroken prairie lands. A year later at least 10 other Swedish immigrant families moved into the region. By 1880, more than 4300 foreign-born Swedes were living in the surrounding lands of Goodhue County.

The centerpiece of their lives and their community was the Swedish Lutheran Church. They responded favorably to the strong leadership of the first Swedish pastor there, the Rev. Eric Norelius. He arrived in 1855 at Vasa, which became the mother community. By 1869 the congregation had built the church now standing there, one of Minnesota's finest immigrant buildings, Vasa Lutheran. Somewhat Greek Revival in style, Vasa shows distinctive Swedish architectural overtones. Nearby stands the parish museum, which has a fine collection of historical memorabilia. Norelius was a church planter, organizing the two congregations (among several others) seen on this tour: St. Ansgar's Lutheran in 1870 and Spring Garden in 1869.

Most of the first two generations of Swedish immigrants remained in farming and related occupations. As their numbers grew and opportunities for more specialized careers opened, the children moved to the larger cities, especially Minneapolis, which today is a major center for Swedish-American culture. As you ride through the area, note the ongoing pride in owning and directing one's livelihood, namely by farming. Farming methods, crops, and buildings have all changed. What has remained constant is what was discovered by all three immigrant groups: By becoming landowners in America they created opportunities for their own advancement and for the future of their children in ways they would never have known in their home countries. This work ethic, discovered by each ethnic group on the advancing frontiers, served the Swedes well, as you'll see.

To park, go to Cannon Falls and find the downtown intersection of MN 19, MN 20, and CR 24, about 0.5 mile east of US 52 (Cannon Falls exit). One block west of the intersection you'll find the parking lot, which is also the lot for Tours 2 and 23.

0.0 *On leaving the lot, turn left (east) onto MN 19, crossing Main Street.*

You'll pass several local churches.

1.4 *Find St. Ansgar's Lutheran Church on your left.*

The original church was built in 1870, and was named for the patron saint of Sweden. It is a major hub for town and country life.

1.5 *Back on MN 19, continue east.*

This road mostly parallels the Cannon Valley Trail (Tour 2). It is hilly, but the scenery is lovely and the shoulders are ample. Yard art abounds.

8.1 *Pass a Swiss model farm.*

9.7 *Enter Vasa, seeing the church just ahead.*

10.0 *You've arrived at the church parking lot.*

This complex of buildings merits a serious walk-through; see the high-church features and the cemetery. Find the nearby museum, which also has water and picnic tables.

10.2 *Return to MN 19; turn south onto CR 7.*

Note the breadloaf-shaped haystacks and immaculate farms.

13.5 *Turn right (west) onto CR 1 here.*

14.0 *Stay on CR 1.*

Vasa Church

Note the signs for 4-H clubs, evidence of the continuing appeal of farming among young people. And the trees are gorgeous.

19.3 Arrive at the third church, Spring Garden Lutheran Church, today continuing to flourish.

Note the Swedish word *Kyrkan* (church), the stained-glass windows, and the well-kept lawns. It too is the social and religious center of the nearby community.

19.4 Turn right (north) onto CR 25.

24.2 Note such touches as unusually well-trimmed trees, and wash on the line.

25.4 Be ready for a steep descent, running for over a mile.

27.5 CR 25 ends here. Ride right onto CR 24.

28.2 You're back in downtown Cannon Falls and back at your car.

Bicycle Repair Service

Trail Station Sports, 106 Fourth Street North, Cannon Falls; 507-263-5055 or 1-888-835-BIKE

25

Slavic Heritage

Distance: *34.9 miles*
Terrain: *Flat to gently rolling; easy, open country traffic*
Location: *Le Sueur and Rice Counties*
Special features: *Three churches, small-town ambience, farms*

Each migrating ethnic group sought to do two things: first, to preserve the mother country culture, language, religion, food, and social norms, and, second, to be successful American citizens. Immigrants saw no real contradictions in those aims. Since America was the land of the free, why couldn't they recreate their own homelands so long as they obeyed the laws and left others alone?

During the 1850s and 1860s, a large number of families of Czech and Slovak origin came to the United States, many moving directly to Minnesota farmlands. They settled in ethnic enclaves and started life anew.

The Czech and Slovak people (hereafter referred to as Slavic) re-created their homelands in every major way, including religious life. Of central importance was the arrival of European-trained priests and nuns, who were instrumental in launching the Roman Catholic churches. Those you visit within the towns served as outreach ministries to the larger communities. Perhaps as long if not longer than other similar immigrant groups, the Slavic people held on strongly to their heritage.

Today the signs of major change are everywhere. Some Protestant churches are appearing. High-tech agribusiness has replaced the old-time silos and mills. Public and private schools continue to expand. And the three cities visited here try to attract new settlers, not necessarily Slavic.

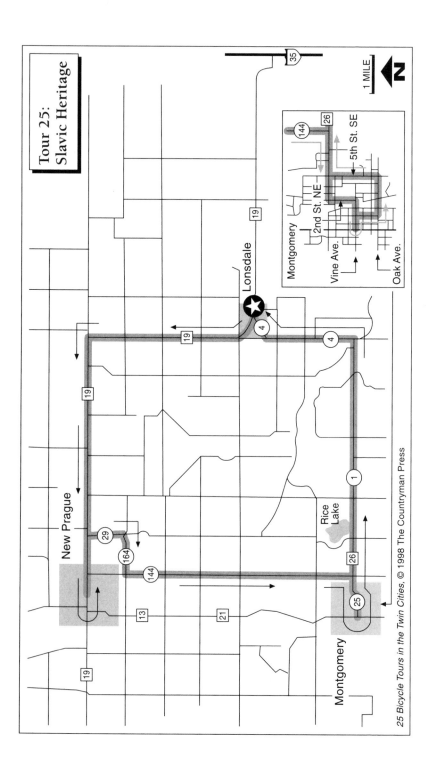

Tour 25:
Slavic Heritage

Lonsdale

New Prague

Montgomery

Rice Lake

Montgomery

2nd St. NE

5th St. SE

Vine Ave.

Oak Ave.

N

1 MILE

25 Bicycle Tours in the Twin Cities, © 1998 The Countryman Press

At the center of each town is the church. With unique Slavic touches in architecture and decoration, these remind the visitors of the stability and ongoing traditional identity of the cities' past. But they serve as more than museums; each has active social outreach, cooperation with other community social agencies, and openness to non-Slavic members. In each instance, you are invited to walk around these towns and churches.

To park, take exit 69 off I-35. Turn west onto MN 19 and drive the 9 miles to Lonsdale. Park at Immaculate Conception Church at the cross streets of Alabama Street SE and First Avenue, just off MN 19. Ride out from there.

0.0 *Turn left (west) onto MN 19 and cross over Main Street.*

As you turn west you'll see the city baseball field. Many small towns nearby have such a structure, their own "field of dreams." Sunday baseball in organized leagues is taken seriously.

0.4 *MN 19 heads north into the open country, with good shoulders for riding.*

2.8 *On the left, note Veseli Church, a rural Catholic parish with a fascinating Italian Renaissance design.*

5.0 *MN 19 bends to the left (west).*

9.0 *Find a United Methodist Church here.*

9.9 *See the Assembly of God Church.*

10.4 *Proceed directly into New Prague.*

11.4 *Locate Main Street, also MN 19, in New Prague.*

11.6 *You'll find facilities at a pleasant city park.*

11.8 *Arrive at St. Wenceslaus Catholic Church, a masterpiece.*

Definitely worth a dismount so you can walk around, this is as close to a major cathedral as you will find outside a metropolitan area. It is the mother church for miles around. Note the elegant baroque touches throughout the sanctuary.

11.9 *Back on your machine, ride west on Main Street and arrive at Schumacher's Restaurant, on your left at the corner of Main Street and Second Avenue SW.*

This is an immensely popular combination of Czech and German high cuisine, and a place for lodging. The owners have furnished

St. Wenceslaus Church in New Prague

12 bedrooms, each representing a month of the year, with authentic appointments from eastern Europe. It is a genuine slice of Slavic life.

12.3 *Make a U-turn here, head east on Main Street, and retrace your way in.*

Note the grand frescoes and murals on the buildings, depicting local history and personalities.

14.0 *Turn right onto CR 29 and ride south out of town.*

14.3 *Turn right (west) onto CR 164.*

16.3 *Turn left (south) onto CR 144.*

This is a seldom-used but flat and well-constructed road, going very close to grainfields and farms.

22.1 Take a right onto CR 26 to Montgomery.

22.9 This is the "kolachy capital of America," named for a tasty Czech pastry made in abundance here.

23.4 Turn left (south) onto Second Street NE.

Be sure to keep alert for changing street signs, for example, NW to SW, or NE to NW.

23.7 Turn right (west) onto Vine Avenue.

This is the heart of town, with restaurants, meat markets, and street banners. At First and Vine, find Holy Redeemer Catholic Church, worth a careful look.

23.8 Turn right (south) onto Second Street SW.

23.9 Turn left (east) onto Oak Avenue SW.

24.2 Turn left (north) onto Fifth Street SE.

25.1 Turn right (east) onto CR 26.

26.0 Find Rice Lake.

Some 10 lakes in Minnesota have the same name.

26.7 The "new" Slavic community is on display here, with several elegant new homes and extensive flower gardens.

27.3 Note CR 26 ends, and CR 1 begins; ride onto CR 1.

31.4 Turn left (north) onto CR 4.

33.8 In Lonsdale, turn right onto MN 19.

34.9 You're back at your car.

Bicycle Repair Service

Dave's Bike Shop, 13753 Echo Avenue, Lonsdale, 507-663-9734

Let Backcountry Guides Take You There

More Biking Guides

In New England and the Northeast
25 Bicycle Tours in Maine
25 Mountain Bike Tours in Massachusetts
25 Bicycle Tours on Cape Cod and the Islands
25 Mountain Bike Tours in Vermont
25 Bicycle Tours in Vermont
25 Mountain Bike Tours in the Hudson Valley
25 Bicycle Tours in the Hudson Valley
25 Bicycle Tours in the Finger Lakes
25 Bicycle Tours in the Adirondacks
The Mountain Biker's Guide to Ski Resorts

In the Mid-Atlantic States
25 Bicycle Tours in Maryland
25 Bicycle Tours on Delmarva
25 Bicycle Tours in Eastern Pennsylvania
30 Bicycle Tours in New Jersey
25 Mountain Bike Tours in New Jersey
25 Bicycle Tours in and around Washington, D.C.

Farther South, Farther West
25 Bicycle Tours in Ohio's Western Reserve
25 Bicycle Tours in Southern Indiana
30 Bicycle Tours in Wisconsin
25 Bicycle Tours in Coastal Georgia and the Carolina Low Country
25 Bicycle Tours in the Texas Hill Country and West Texas

We offer many more books on hiking, fly fishing, travel, nature, and other subjects. Our books are available at bookstores and outdoor stores everywhere. For more information or a free catalog, please call 1-800-245-4151 or write to us at The Countryman Press, PO Box 748, Woodstock, Vermont 05091. You can find us on the Internet at www.countrymanpress.com.